"Questioning the logic—and the orthodoxy—of contemporary fads, Darsey challenges us to anchor our musical and liturgical practices in the historic tradition of the church, innovating in ways that continue to honor and speak out of the centuries-long tradition of Christian worship. This book makes a vital contribution to our reflection on this sacred task."

—DAVID A. DESILVA
Ashland Theological Seminary

The God of Abraham, Isaac, and Jacob

The God of Abraham, Isaac, and Jacob

Music and Worship

STEVEN DARSEY

WIPF & STOCK · Eugene, Oregon

THE GOD OF ABRAHAM, ISAAC, AND JACOB
Music and Worship

Copyright © 2013 Steven Darsey. All rights reserved. Except for brief quotations in critical publications or reviews, no part of this book may be reproduced in any manner without prior written permission from the publisher. Write: Permissions, Wipf and Stock Publishers, 199 W. 8th Ave., Suite 3, Eugene, OR 97401.

Wipf & Stock
An Imprint of Wipf and Stock Publishers
199 W. 8th Ave., Suite 3
Eugene, OR 97401
www.wipfandstock.com

ISBN 13: 978-1-62032-730-2
Manufactured in the U.S.A.

Biblical citations are from the New Revised Standard Version Bible, copyright 1989, Division of Christian Education of the National Council of the Churches of Christ in the United States of America. Used by permission. All rights reserved.

"The Secret Sits" and excerpt from "Birches" from the book THE POETRY OF ROBERT FROST edited by Edward Connery Lathem. Copyright © 1916, 1969 by Henry Holt and Company, copyright © 1942, 1944 by Robert Frost, copyright © 1970 by Lesley Frost Ballantine. Reprinted by arrangement with Henry Holt and Company, LLC.

Photographs throughout the book were taken by Steven Darsey ©, 2012, in various sections of the United States.

Contents

Guest Preface ix
Preface xv
Poem: Cantate Domino xix

1 Language of Worship 1
2 Prophecy or Idolatry 5
3 Holiness in Worship 10
4 Holiness in Music 18
5 Church Music Midrash 32
6 Church Music Canon 40
7 Pastoral Leadership 47
8 Making Decisions 56
9 Misconceptions 65
10 God First 83

Bibliography 91

Guest Preface

Guest Preface

THE READER WILL NOTICE from the outset two qualities of the writer: he knows the subject and he believes it is important. The subject is the worship of God and specifically, the role of music in that worship. Dr. Darsey resists the idea that the choice of that music lies with the senior minister. Church musicians are not called to provide the sound track for the weekly sermon. While the minister in charge has the authority to say the final word in matters of liturgy and music, he or she is often unprepared to do so. As a result, it is often the case that the minister simply notifies the minister of music what the sermon topic is and maybe a hymn to go with it. It would be immensely helpful if the minister had training in music for worship but such training is in the curriculum of few seminaries. There are courses in preaching and properly so, but much more is happening on Sunday morning than a word from the pulpit.

In fact, says Dr. Darsey, very often too much is going on in the service of worship. Pressure is put on the service to make room for announcements of upcoming events, promotion of community projects, and all manner of parish business. After all, more members are present in worship than at any other time, so what better occasion for pushing the youth pumpkin sale to raise money for the ski trip to Aspen? Cut out one hymn and the service will still conclude by noon. Of course, these are matters of importance in the life of the church but surely there are other times and places appropriate.

And then there are voices raised promoting a praise service. Why? Other churches have them. Following worship in a church where I was a guest preacher recently, I was asked if I was going to stay for the praise service. I replied, "I thought that is what we just had. We praised God." But I knew what he meant: a screen drops, a forest

Guest Preface

of microphones rise on the chancel, and brief choruses are sung repeatedly. A compromise is struck: insert into the traditional service a few choruses accompanied by a guitar, a banjo, and drums. Perhaps in time the new technology will be baptized.

In the meantime, Dr. Darsey and other church musicians must provide an experience of the presence of God for a worshiping community living in a culture of consumerism, a market driven culture, which asks of the church what it asks of every other store on the block: make me feel good about myself. And church after church submits, not fully aware that they are no longer congregations of faith but audiences waiting to be entertained.

Dr. Darsey knows it is difficult to witness to the transcendence of a sovereign God who for us and our salvation has appeared with forgiving grace. To guide himself and others he turns to the scriptures not only to be reminded that some things are more important than how we happen to feel about them, but also to learn anew how the church historic has maintained its freshness, its liveliness, without simply purchasing a few songs off the rack. Or, to change the image, it is not necessary to chop down the family tree in order to be "contemporary." It is in making a case for church music which is appropriate to the worship of God that Dr. Darsey is at his best. To be sure, he accepts the task of exposing church music that is inadequate and inappropriate, but his major contribution is in identifying and characterizing music that is worthy of the sanctuary. From his discussion, I call attention to three key terms.

Identity. The primary purpose of church music is to set the worshiper before the mystery of God. Such music does not indulge in expressing feelings about God nor does it give the impression that the composer had walked all around God and taken pictures. God remains a mystery.

Guest Preface

Reverence is aware of distance. Having said that, worthy church music does not allow mystery to be an invitation to fill in the blanks. This is to say, since God is mystery, any object of worship is as good as any other. As one can be in love with love, or have faith in faith, so one might be in awe of awe. For this reason, Dr. Darsey identifies the God we worship as the God of Abraham, Isaac, and Jacob. All other gods are idols.

Memory. Worthy church music has memory. By memory, Dr. Darsey is not referring to recall, or recognition, or even reverie. Rather he means memory in the biblical sense of entering into the life and experience of our faith forebears. For example, a Jewish child might say on a sacred evening, "We were in Egypt and we were sore oppressed, but God heard our cry and brought us out with a strong arm and mighty hand."[1] This child is twelve years old and has never been out of Detroit, but she remembers, she enters into the tragedy and the deliverance of her people. So church music remembers, all the way back to Eden, and to God, and to the one fundamental human longing, the longing for God. "Sometimes I feel like a motherless child, a long way from home."[2]

Canon. Until I read this book I had never thought of canon as referring to anything other than the scriptures, a collection of writings that serve as an authoritative guide for the life of a believing community. Could there be a collection of church music which serves as an authoritative guide for Christian worship? Dr. Darsey would have us ponder it. How did certain writings achieve the status of scripture?

---

1. Paraphrase of Deut. 6:21.

2. Quote from the African American spiritual, "Sometimes I Feel Like a Motherless Child," anonymous.

Guest Preface

By wide and continuous use in the churches, some writings were judged to be of the Holy Spirit while others were not. Decisions were not hasty nor were they unanimous, but eventually the church had her book. The closing of the canon served to give the church stability while the continued interpretation of the writings gave flexibility; in other words, kept them current or "contemporary." A few years ago, a friend joined my wife and me for an evening of Mozart under the direction of Robert Shaw of the Atlanta Symphony. Our friend, being a musician, brought his copies of Mozart with him and followed the symphony carefully. He expressed appreciation for the concert and commented on a few surprises in the performance. I asked him if every musician was free to render Mozart according to personal preferences and he said, "No, we always have the music" as he patted his folder.

Do we have, or are we in the process of having a canon of church music which will provide the worshiping community both stability and flexibility?

Dr. Darsey has my attention with this important book.

Fred B. Craddock
Bandy Distinguished Professor of Preaching
and New Testament, Emeritus,
Candler School of Theology, Emory University

Preface

Preface

"Now we have received not the spirit of the world, but the Spirit that is from God, so that we may understand the gifts bestowed on us by God. And we speak of these things in words not taught by human wisdom but taught by the Spirit, interpreting spiritual things to those who are spiritual" (1 Cor 2:12–13).

On the den wall of my grandparents' home in Charlotte, North Carolina, there hung a picture of the Men's Bible Class of the Hawthorne Lane United Methodist Church. My grandmother played the piano for the class and my grandfather led the singing. In the picture, there were some one hundred men standing in front of the church. I have seen such pictures from many different churches depicting Sunday school classes, church choirs, and congregations over-brimming with members. Most of these pictures lamentably come from earlier times—times when virtually everyone went to church.

Now the picture is different. Classes, choirs, and congregations are smaller. Many people no longer attend church. Diminished numbers have church leaders, with the psalmist, asking the gnawing question, "My God, why have you forsaken me?" In my now forty years as a practicing church musician, I have lived through the anxious search for the mysterious formula that will bring the crowds back. While this search seems of particular relevance to my era, the means of bringing the world to Christ have been and will likely always be of critical importance to the church. The search goes on.

As has been true throughout the church's history, possibilities arise from many quarters. Welcome proposals have been vaunted for all arenas of church administration and ministry. My concern is with those designed to increase attendance by making dramatic changes in our tradition of worship, especially as they affect music. We know

Preface

from scripture and from doctors of the church that how we worship is of critical import, affecting the very character of our faith and our relation to God. The courses some churches are choosing, their reasons for doing so, and the consequences I believe these portend, along with the love I feel for the church of Christ have inspired me to share some ideas, particularly on church music. These I hope might be of help to churches making future decisions. While I am responding to issues of my time, I have tried to look, not solely at the presenting circumstances, but to their underlying philosophies, in the hope that these recommendations might be relevant now and in the future.

To understand the role of music in worship, one must first address worship; and so in the ensuing chapters I share my views of worship, propose some ideas on the role of music in worship (some of which I believe to be new), challenge some worship practices, address what I see as systemic problems productive of error, and propose solutions. It has been my goal to assume the best intentions for all. Should any of these ideas be found controversial, I hope they do not give offense.

I am not ordained clergy, nor am I degreed in liturgy or theology. By calling and training, I am a church musician. I was bred in the United Methodist church and have been privileged to serve in several denominations. As a lifelong church member, employee, and worship leader, and as a frequent attender of worship as a congregant, I have had opportunity to help plan, lead, and participate in many services. These have given me the opportunity to observe and draw conclusions.

I acknowledge my debt to theologian Marva Dawn, whose prophetic insight and courage have shown the way for many, and to others, some named in the ensuing pages, most unmentioned, who have generously nurtured my

Preface

work and understanding. I express particular gratitude to Gary Hauk, David deSilva, Deborah Marlowe, and Jane Thorpe for substantive advice and to Fred Craddock for his prescient wisdom.

I believe worship to be the most important human endeavor and the church's signal responsibility. I offer no magic formulae, no quick fixes, and no promises of great numbers and wealth. I offer what I hope is common spiritual sense: that if through simple commitment, hard work and sincere faith, we put and keep our worship houses in order and thereby draw near to God, God will send us the Holy Spirit, renew the vitality of our churches and the strength of our faith, and draw near to us. To gain our bearings, we look to the ways of our forebears.

Cantate Domino

Two ventured forth to worship God.
One cast his praise in worldly lays;
One, scripture awed, narrow trod.
Each found success, but holiness
Does not essay all human ways.
Who does the path of God confess?

Cantate Domino is the fruit of a suggestion by Fred Craddock that
I write a poem to introduce the book, which I did in May of 2008.

1

Language of Worship

For Christ was in the world, but not of the world.[1]

---

1. This phrase is commonly used as if it were scriptural, though it is actually an aphorism distilled from John 17:13–16.

The God of Abraham, Isaac, and Jacob

WE ARE ON A timeless journey with and toward God. We strive to know and serve God, and long for the utility and beauty of living in harmony with God's will. Coveting this relationship, we search for ways of sharing it with those who don't know it, we search for ways to increase it for those who do, and we search to deepen it for ourselves.

> *We dance round in a ring and suppose,*
> *But the Secret sits in the middle and knows.*[2]

God is omnipresent. God is with us everywhere, and at all times, beyond place and time. "Where can I go from your spirit? Or where can I flee from your presence"? (Ps 139:7). Of all times and places, however, the time and place of high worship, where humans and God covenant to meet in mutual respect, is *sui generis*: the most fecund, the *sine qua non* of the divine-human relationship. There, by mutual consent, we grow in God and God grows in us.

Thus, embodied in and commanded by scripture, and in accord with our deepest instincts, we choose a time and place to worship God in the spirit of holiness, where we maintain our relationship and share mutual love in a committed, disciplined manner. Humans offer their very best on these occasions; and God responds by sharing the scripture, the Holy Spirit, divine guidance and wisdom. There, we also feel the awe and ineffable joy of being in the presence of God, in the beauty of holiness. "I will be your God and you will be my people" (Jer 30:22).

From the dawn of human consciousness, humans have been worshiping God under this mutual covenant. Divine revelations have invoked changes in our understanding of the nature of God and of the practice of our religions; but the liturgy of worship, though manifesting itself in myriad forms over the centuries—truly practiced—has evolved

2. Frost, "Secret Sits," 362.

Language of Worship

from ancient times in this unbroken dialectical relationship in worship with God.

Through this worship covenant, over the centuries, God and humanity have developed a common language, a language that, granting human limitations and God's unreachable height, nevertheless enables communication and a growing understanding and relationship. This language is in part didactic, as in scripture and hymns; in part artistic, as in music, art, and architecture; in part communal, for it is done in the presence of others and God; and in part spiritual, as expressed in contemplation and prayer. Each has its unique, essential utility and historic role in divine-human communication, and in combination, they comprise our ongoing language of worship. "His voice was like the sound of many waters" (Rev 1:15).

Thus, evolving in the divine precincts of worship, this is the language by which God and humans recognize and know each other. It is the unique language of worship and is therefore distinct from and alien to the language of the world. There we may learn and practice the secrets unknown to the world that Paul describes in his first letter to the Corinthians.

> But we speak God's wisdom, secret and hidden, which God decreed before the ages for our glory . . . So also no one comprehends what is truly God's except the Spirit of God. Now we have received not the spirit of the world, but the Spirit that is from God, so that we may understand the gifts bestowed on us by God. And we speak of these things in words not taught by human wisdom but taught by the Spirit, interpreting spiritual things to those who are spiritual. Those who are unspiritual do not receive the gifts of God's Spirit, for they are foolishness to them, and they

> are unable to understand them because they are spiritually discerned. (1 Cor 2:7–14)

In the ensuing chapters, I will address means of advancing this shared language and relationship through the art of music.

2

Prophecy or Idolatry

The God of Abraham, Isaac, and Jacob. (Exod 3:6)

The God of Abraham, Isaac, and Jacob

WHILE A STUDENT OF sacred music at Yale in the early 1980s, I was privileged to serve as Assistant Music Director for the Church of Christ at Yale. Among my duties was attendance at weekly staff meetings. This was an honor, for I considered every moment in the presence of Chaplain John Vannorsdall ennobling. I was always asking prodigious questions in staff meetings, like "What does it mean that Jesus died for our sins?" He may have dreaded these, but he never showed it and always patiently answered them. Once I asked him why biblical prayers are often addressed to "the God of Abraham, Isaac, and Jacob," and the like, rather than simply to God. He said they were identifying the God to whom they were praying. This struck me profoundly.

This meant that it was also possible to pray to the wrong god. If it's possible to pray to the wrong god, it's possible to address the wrong god in worship—a practice called idolatry. We well know this practice as condemned by biblical prophets, but rarely do we consider that we might practice it ourselves today. Idolatry, however, is alive and well.

Which of today's liturgical practices might the prophets identify as idolatrous? If we were practicing idolatry, how would we know it? Stating it positively, how do we ensure that our worship is addressing the God of Abraham, Isaac, and Jacob, and not another god? Marva Dawn, in *Reaching Out Without Dumbing Down: A Theology of Worship for This Urgent Time*, makes clear that everything in worship should be directed to God, and that worship components directed otherwise, however worthily intended, are idolatrous.[1] How do we avoid this?

Remembering John Vannorsdall's answer above, we could simply state this before our prayers and spoken acts

---

1. Dawn, *Reaching Out*, 80–87.

Prophecy or Idolatry

of liturgy. But what about other liturgical elements—among them, movement, dance, art, paraments, vestments, architecture, and music? How do we identify the god we are addressing through these media? In music, for example, how do we ensure that our voluntaries, anthems, and hymns are directed to the God of Abraham, Isaac, and Jacob?

On Easter of 2006, my church, Glenn Memorial United Methodist Church (UMC), was blessed with the preaching of Fred B. Craddock. Preparing music to honor the occasion and the high character of his preaching was a blessed challenge. After learning the scripture and the general content of his sermon, I began to look for just the right music to match his sermon and the needs of our congregation as I understood them for this all-important service. I couldn't find just the right thing, so I decided I had to compose an anthem: a heavy responsibility to place upon oneself for this great day. Where does one go to find the right ideas to express textually and musically for Easter Sunday? I had the scripture and sermon theme and was able to find a text from the Psalms that would work well with the sermon. It's hard to go wrong with a psalm, but what of the music?

I thought of the important twentieth-century composer Maurice Duruflé, who used Gregorian chant as the foundation for most of his choral music. From this basis, he added melodic ideas and harmonies from his own creative palette. *Thus he built on a foundation of words and melodies that had been sung for centuries by his Christian forebears,* and brought these into contemporary liturgical parlance via his compositional genius. By quoting text and tune from the ancient Christian liturgy—a musical time-tag ID—he made it unequivocally clear that he was addressing the God of Abraham, Isaac, and Jacob.

Even for an inveterate United Methodist like myself, Duruflé makes a good model, so I looked to the historic

The God of Abraham, Isaac, and Jacob

Catholic liturgies and found two chants, one from Ascension Sunday, "Psallite Dominus," and another from Easter, "Surrexit Dominus." I quoted these two chants literally and composed supporting music and included some additional words in English from Psalm 68, from which comes the text for "Psallite." While it does not compare to Duruflé, the use of these two time-honored chants made me feel more confident that the piece I presented would have the right things to say, would be theologically and musically appropriate, and would address the God of Abraham, Isaac, and Jacob. I am grateful that it was well received.

Of course, not all churches can or want to sing Duruflé motets for worship. However, these principles operate in music at all levels of musical complexity. For example, the hymn, "O Come, O Come, Emmanuel," is an example, like Duruflé, where an ancient chant is obviously adapted for congregational singing, and, less obviously, "My Faith Looks Up to Thee," often sung to the tune HAMBURG, was arranged by Lowell Mason from an ancient chant tune. These hymns are commonly sung in American Christian parishes of many denominations.

We are enjoined in the Psalms to "sing to the Lord a new song" (Ps 96:1). Certainly we need and want a progression of new music to explore our evolving relationship with God. However, while we want new music, we do not want new gods.

How do we direct new songs to the God of our forebears? We have Duruflé for one fine example, but we certainly are not limited to quoting chant. There is no sure formula, for the ways of God are beyond mortal ken; but there are guideposts. *My philosophy holds that new music written for worship should partake of and commend itself to the inherited musical tradition of the church—to our inherited language of worship.* Therefore, one hedges against

Prophecy or Idolatry

idolatry by choosing worship materials that are bred in or relate dynamically to the ancient traditions of the church.

Stating it negatively, one risks idolatry by choosing materials from outside the tradition of the church—by choosing materials from and vaunted by the world; for example, music whose textual and musical styles derive from popular culture: songs whose melodic contours, rhythmic patterns, harmonic language, chordal structure, and affective "hooks" derive from any of the many popular styles of music. Secular music is important, worthy high art and is justifiably beloved and ideal for its purposes; but just as Gregorian chant cannot work for a square dance, popular styled music, in general, is not efficacious for worship. I say "in general," because there are geniuses; for example, Duke Ellington, who has written music using popular idioms that is undeniably sacred. Nevertheless granting such exceptions, *understanding the genealogy of the musical style, as evolving either from the church or from popular culture, is a critical first step in discerning a given musical selection's propriety for worship and the god it addresses.* This genealogical measure is important, of course, not just for music, but also for all elements of liturgy.

Of course God does speak through new music; but we must remember that not all that's new is of God—"beware false prophets" (Matt 7:15). Biblical prophecies show fidelity to the will of God against the temptations of popular culture. Therefore when new worship styles and music speak from and for the world over and against biblical-liturgical tradition, they should be scrutinized as possible false prophecies. When we compose new songs that are bred in, founded on, and extend from the evolving musical voice of the Church—part of the unique language of the divine-human relationship—rather than other gods, we may hope to address the God of Abraham, Isaac, and Jacob.

3

Holiness in Worship

*Remember the Sabbath day, and keep it holy.
(Exod 20:8)*

Holiness in Worship

WE HAVE ALL BEEN awestruck in nature—seeing a rare, beautiful creature, or, after an arduous hike, a spectacular scene that takes our breath and overwhelms our souls with the glory of creation. Such numinous experiences make us feel we are standing on holy ground. Some ancient civilizations found holy ground in caves, where they built temples and felt the divine presence in the fathomless dark, and heard God speak in the mysterious ringing echoes. Others built their sanctuaries in above-ground caves that we call mounds and still others did so and called them cathedrals, churches, and meeting houses. In these, holy echoes yet ring. Though their architectural styles range from austere simplicity to artful complexity, they were built on ground believed to be holy and designed as sanctuaries where God is invited to dwell. Creeds, liturgies and practices may differ, but all need this sanctuary—a refuge from the vicissitudes of the world and place where, when entered, the spirit of God may be found.

As Solomon was commanded to build a house for the holy of holies, so we too are charged to offer a sanctuary for the worship of God. We know that to become manifest and to communicate at any time or place, via any means, are among God's prerogatives and blessings for humanity. While we are open to and grateful for these wherever and whenever they may be offered, we nevertheless respond in gratitude by building a holy sanctuary, by making and honoring appointments to worship, and there, by offering God our highest praise.

In *The Interpreter's Dictionary of the Bible,* James Muilenburg includes this statement on holiness: "Its connotations are as diverse as the cultures which seek to describe its mysterious nature, but common to all is an awareness of an undefined and uncanny energy, a sense of the numinous (cf. Latin *numen*), of the imponderable and incomprehensible, an inarticulate feeling of an inviolable potency outside and beyond, removed and distant, yet at the same time near and 'fascinating,' invading the everyday world of normal experience—what Rudolf Otto has described as the *mysterium tremendum*."[1]

Why has God enjoined us to keep the Sabbath holy? We are given this commandment because God knows we need time apart from the world—time in the distinct presence of God—sometimes alone in nature, sometimes in solitary prayer, but also time with the community of believers. When we humans take the initiative, as individuals or as a faith community, we approach the holy of holies by leaving the human world and entering the realm of God.

> O Lord of all, though you have need of nothing,
> you were pleased that there should be a temple
> for your habitation among us. (2 Macc 14:35).

How do we create such a place? From the long divine-human history of structures we have many models. My ideal would have the sanctuary designed and treated differently from all other buildings and places. Where this space has to be shared with other activities, then steps would be taken to invoke appropriate holiness before and during high times of worship. The space, to the extent possible, would be made to look, sound, and feel like a habitation for God, and therefore unlike those of humans. It could be a little apart, suggesting God's transcendence, and so that the approach requires some extra effort—a degree of sacrifice.

The sanctuary would be approached with a respect appropriate to its holiness. Whether or not appropriate music is being offered, the sanctuary should be entered in silence,

1. Muilenburg, "Holiness," 616.

Holiness in Worship

with the expectation that God is present and ready to communicate with those with ears to hear. "Let me hear what God the Lord will speak" (Ps 85:8). "But the Lord is in his holy temple; let all the earth keep silence before him!" (Hab 2:20). Other than congregational confessions, responses, and hymns, this expectant, fecund, holy silence should be maintained throughout the entire service, until the congregant leaves the sanctuary and returns to the world.

Every liturgical item offered would be chosen for and executed with the aim of enabling communion between the people and God. Each act of worship would be offered with a distant formality—an anonymity—where the individual leaders and congregants surrender their egos to the liturgy itself, invoking and encouraging the Holy Spirit to expand its presence in each successive act of worship so that the congregation is drawn ever more deeply into communion with God. The formality of worship enables leaders and congregants to surrender their personal needs to the liturgy. Thus, personal greetings, silly jokes, offhand remarks, and other informalities would be left for other occasions, and every act, word spoken, and note sung are offered, even if lighthearted or humorous, with a consideration appropriate to the gravity of worship.

Pastoral concerns may be handled formally before and during prayers. Otherwise, there would be no announcements, no congregational business, no time of greeting each other, no applause for our accomplishments—absolutely nothing that interferes with the solemn, though vital, progression of the liturgy and the congregation's communion with God.

For example: individuals enter the sanctuary before the service in silence. While sitting in reverence before the Almighty, or listening to an opening voluntary and apprehending the beauty of the sanctuary, they open their souls

The God of Abraham, Isaac, and Jacob

to the holiness of the space and to the movement of the Holy Spirit. They are quickened by a call to worship and then join their sisters and brothers in an opening hymn, where the Spirit, joined by the music, swells among and unites the congregants spiritually, building momentum into the ensuing prayer, and growing steadily through each subsequent act of liturgy, until, reaching its climax in the final prayer, it sends the faithful forth, full of faith and glory for sharing Christ with the world. Only if the formality and holiness of the liturgy proceeds uninterrupted may the Holy Spirit grow to its greatest strength and ideally work God's transfiguring grace in our souls.

Done rightly, this would not lead to cold or dispassionate liturgies. Worship leaders, through appropriate decorum, show conviction, love, and joy in their offerings, and the readings, prayers, sermon, and music are chosen, composed, and delivered with the complete spectrum of expression, from quiet simplicity, through joyful abandon, to stunning passion.

Such an approach to worship is rarely undertaken, for among even those few worship leaders who agree in principle, most believe it impractical or impossible to implement. Many churches confuse worship with other important components of ministry, principally evangelism and fellowship. These are essential ministries of any Christian church, but, even though some insist otherwise, they are not acts of worship.

Because we recognize that God rejoices when we share our faith with others and when we share fellowship and love with our Christian sisters and brothers, we confuse these with acts of worship. Not all good things are acts of worship. Not even all godly things are acts of worship. For example, installing church plumbing or rehearsing church choirs are good and, at best, godly endeavors, and are essential to the

Holiness in Worship

ministry of the church, but they are not acts of worship and do not belong in our worship services. Putting them there not only weakens our worship, but diminishes the sum of all our ministries. Our worship services should be solely worship and include nothing else.

This does not mean, however, that worship is devoid of fellowship, for true worship is rich in fellowship: we read, listen, pray, and sing communally. Doing these in worship under the providence of the Holy Spirit enables us to grow together in fellowship with each other and with God. This is a holy communion possible only through worship, and is far deeper and more spiritual than the glad-handing interpersonal greetings—welcome in other church settings—too often practiced in worship in the name of Christian fellowship. This, though unintentionally, displaces the focus of worship from God to ourselves.

Many in my own and other ecclesial traditions speak more for the immanence than the transcendence of God in worship, or if they want to observe both, don't want the vertical (God centered) to exclude the horizontal (people centered). I believe, however, that the vertical is what we most need in the one high hour of worship that most of us observe weekly. We have the rest of the week and the panoply of other church ministries to observe the immanent—the horizontal. Just as we as individuals need time alone with God, so too do congregations. I fear that many of those worshiping bodies who claim a more immanent theology rarely in actual practice encounter God in worship, and if not then, when? Even those who theoretically account for transcendence in their liturgies often displace time for God with congregational business and interpersonal greetings. Too often, when we think of it at all, we delude ourselves into believing our worship is of God when

The God of Abraham, Isaac, and Jacob

it is merely a succession of acts focused (unintentionally) on ourselves that successfully distract us from attending to God. Individuals who don't take time to ruminate, to ponder, to consider, and pray alone with God, tend to lack depth. Congregations who fail to spend such time in communal worship focused on God also risk being spiritually shallow.

Not everything has to be baldly stated or acted out. God sent Christ into the world, not as a terrible monarch, but as a humble carpenter, and the world knew him not. The African American spiritual-styled song says, "we didn't know who you was."[2] As God was incarnate in Jesus, but initially unrecognized, so, though our worship focuses on God—transcendence, Christ is nevertheless incarnate and manifest—immanence. When we honor the transcendent—the Godhead—we also honor the immanent, and our hearts, full of the knowledge of God, are also filled with the love of Christ, the Holy Spirit, and our neighbors. Leaving the precincts of worship, with souls full of our transcendent God, we carry the love of Christ into the world.

Understandably, we want to practice other ministries when our people are gathered for worship, for this is when we can reach them most easily. However, non-worship interjections break the flow of the Holy Spirit and weaken the spiritual potency of the service. God needs our attention in order to communicate. We must attend so that God can give us what we need. If we don't actually worship at the one time a week that most people gather for this purpose, we have missed our most solemn responsibility and our most joyful opportunity to be in the presence of God.

As Marva Dawn relates, anything in worship whose *raison d'être* is to attract people, bring in income, or increase the prestige and power of worship leaders and churches, no

2. MacGimsey, "Sweet Little Jesus Boy."

Holiness in Worship

matter its style, is idolatry.[3] We have made an idol of being "friendly" in worship. God is jealous of our worship and will not brook our focus on other matters. "You shall have no other gods before me" (Exod 20:3).

Should we put the worship of God first, God will rejoice and bless not only our worship, but all other ministries as well. Though challenging, we can nevertheless find ways of effectively practicing evangelism, fellowship, and other ministries outside of worship.

Though unusual, this approach is not some theoretical, practically unattainable liturgical dream, for I have been in a congregation that, while simultaneously practicing the full panoply of churchly ministries, lived this worship discipline successfully. This was not a high Anglican, but rather a Southern Baptist congregation. Silence and awe before the Almighty are not sole provinces in worship of any denomination or liturgical tradition and can be practiced with authenticity by all faith traditions, and there are many churches that do this well. Withal, it is biblical, and helps ensure that we are addressing the God of Abraham, Isaac, and Jacob.

We as individuals and our societies across the world need more than ever to give the Holy Spirit free reign and to give God full voice, so that we may hear and carry the truth of Christ unto the ends of the world. Were we fully to give our hearts and minds to God in worship, what God, so invited, might do for us, eye hath not seen nor ear heard (1 Cor 2:9).

---

3. Dawn, *Reaching Out*, 41–45.

4

Holiness in Music

Test the spirits to see whether they are from God.
(1 John 4:1)

Holiness in Music

To keep our Sabbath holy, and encounter the *mysterium tremendum* in worship, we make our worship spaces, our liturgies, and the individual components of liturgy holy. Infusing our worship with holiness is a never ending, uncertain, and awe-inspiring responsibility. There is no failsafe formula for success. We may approach this humbling responsibility by first offering what our forebears thought holy and then by creating new components based on the worship traditions they gave us. We do our best to determine whether the character of the liturgical component is appropriate for worship and that it addresses the God of Abraham, Isaac, and Jacob.

Among the most ancient and powerful of liturgical arts is music. That music is a holy gift of God is confirmed many places in the Bible and by historic church leaders. Consider this statement from Fred B. Craddock.

> Music is woven into the life of the world. The natives of Australia say God sang the world into being. African Americans say God was humming and patting his foot when he created the world. Jewish people say morning stars sang together, the hills danced, and the trees clapped their hands. A 10-month old baby in a high chair pouring oatmeal on its head, hears a lively tune on the radio, and begins to move to its beat.
>
> Music is a mystery. Trace its origin and you arrive at God. Music bears our griefs and carries our sorrows. Music lulls the child to sleep, sends the soldier into battle, raises the poor from the ground, shakes the thrones of the mighty, galvanizes a community, and sets us all before God.[1]

---

1. Craddock, "Appalachian Weekend."

The God of Abraham, Isaac, and Jacob

FOUNDATIONS FOR HOLINESS IN MUSIC

Wisdom from Our Church Forebears

Honoring music in worship is a sacred duty. Keeping it holy, in the character of the literature selected and in the style of performance, has been an important consideration throughout the church's history. The following quotations show the importance of keeping the character of music holy and the evil consequences of not doing so.

Saint John Chrysostom (345–407)

> Inasmuch as this kind of pleasure is thoroughly innate to our mind, and lest demons introducing lascivious songs should overthrow everything, God established the psalms, in order that singing might be both a pleasure and a help. From strange chants, harm, ruin, and many grievous matters are brought in, for those things that are lascivious and vicious in all songs settle in parts of the mind, making it softer and weaker; from the spiritual psalms, however, proceeds much of value, much utility, much sanctity, and every inducement to philosophy, for the words purify the mind and the Holy Spirit descends swiftly upon the mind of the singer. For those who sing with understanding invoke the grace of the Spirit.[2]

---

2. Chrysostom, "Exposition of Psalm XLI," 68.

Holiness in Music

John Calvin (1509–1564)

And in truth we know by experience that song has great force and vigor to move and inflame the hearts of men to invoke and praise God with a more vehement and ardent zeal. It must always be looked to that the song be not light and frivolous but have weight and majesty, as Saint Augustine says, and there is likewise a great difference between the music one makes to entertain men at table and in their homes, and the psalms which are sung in the presence of God and His angels.

Now among the other things proper to recreate man and give him pleasure, music is either the first or one of the principal, and we must think that it is a gift of God deputed to that purpose. For which reason we must be the more careful not to abuse it, for fear of soiling and contaminating it, converting it to our condemnation when it was dedicated to our profit and welfare.... But there is still more, for there is hardly anything in the world with more power to turn or bend, this way and that, the morals of men, as Plato has prudently considered. And in fact we find by experience that it has a secret and almost incredible power to move our hearts in one way or another.

Wherefore we must be the more diligent in ruling it in such a manner that it may be useful to us and in no way pernicious. For this reason the early doctors of the church often complain that the people of their times are addicted to dishonest and shameless songs, which not without reason they call mortal and Satanic poison for

The God of Abraham, Isaac, and Jacob

the corruption of the world. Now in speaking of music I understand two parts, namely, the letter, or subject and matter, and the song, or melody. It is true that, as Saint Paul says, every evil word corrupts good manners, but when it has the melody with it, it pierces the heart much more strongly and enters within; as wine is poured into the cask with a funnel, so venom and corruption are distilled to the very depths of the heart by melody. Now what is there to do? It is to have songs not merely honest but also holy, which will be like spurs to incite us to pray to God and praise Him, and to meditate upon his works in order to love, fear, honor, and glorify Him....

But may the world be so well advised that instead of the songs that it has previously used, in part vain and frivolous, in part stupid and dull, in part foul and vile and consequently evil and harmful, it may accustom itself hereafter to sing these divine and celestial hymns with the good King David. Touching the melody, it has seemed best that it be moderated in the way that we have adopted in order that it may have the weight and majesty proper to the subject that may even be suitable for singing in church, according to what has been said.[3]

Martin Luther (1483–1546)

Next to the Word of God, music deserves the highest praise. She is a mistress and governess

---

3. Calvin, "Epistle to the Reader" from the Genevan Psalter (1543), 346–48.

of those human emotions—to pass over the animals—which as masters govern men or more often, overwhelm them. . . .

And you, my young friend, let this noble, wholesome, and cheerful creation of God [music] be commended to you. By it you may escape shameful desires and bad company. At the same time you may by this creation accustom yourself to recognize and praise the Creator. Take special care to shun perverted minds who prostitute this lovely gift of nature and of art with their erotic rantings; and be quite assured that none but the devil goads them on to defy their very nature, which would and should praise God its Maker with this gift, so that these bastards purloin the gift of God and use it to worship the foe of God, the enemy of nature and of this lovely art.[4]

Pius X (1835–1914)

Sacred music must therefore eminently possess the qualities which belong to liturgical rites, especially holiness and beauty, from which its other characteristic, universality, will follow spontaneously. It must be holy, and therefore avoid everything that is secular, both in itself and in the way it is performed. It must really be an art, since in no other way can it have on the mind of those who hear it that effect which the church desires in using in her liturgy the art of sound.[5]

---

4. Luther, "Martin Luther to the Devotees of Music," 323–24.
5. Pius X, "Instruction on Sacred Music" (1903), 223–24.

The God of Abraham, Isaac, and Jacob

Fidelity to Scripture

Given this power of music for good or ill, it is essential that the church be highly circumspect in its use. To which of the church's musical practices today might these observations apply? Below I list biblical and theological precepts with possible abuses and descriptions of how these may, perhaps unknowingly, be committed.

Put No Other Gods Before Me

Putting other gods before the God of Abraham, Isaac, and Jacob—idolatry—may be committed through the misuse of otherwise benign materials and techniques. Practices that signal possible idolatry include the use of:

1. Music designed by composition and/or performance style to attract worldly gain or fame for the performer or for the church.
2. Words and music that are emotionally or sensually cloying, designed to invoke a cheap affect from the congregation rather than focusing on communion with God.
3. Liturgical items directed to goals other than worshiping God, no matter how worthy (i.e., to attract members, for stewardship, etc.).
4. Music whose style is indistinguishable from music of the world.

Honor Your Father and Mother

When we discard the musical styles and other liturgical forms given us by our forebears, we dishonor our mothers, fathers, and our genetic and spiritual forebears and break this commandment.

Keep the Sabbath Holy

When we offer music and other liturgical elements that are not holy, we break this commandment.

Offer an Acceptable Sacrifice to God

When we offer liturgical acts that use words and music whose lack of skill, art, and sacrifice in composition render it inappropriate as an offering to God, we offer an unacceptable sacrifice. King David said, "I will not offer burnt-offerings to the Lord my God that cost me nothing" (2 Sam 24:24).

Fidelity to Church Doctrine

Arian Heresy

We each have a natural desire for a God who is our associate, our friend. One who is comfortable, pleasant, and even fun to be with—one who is just like us. As attractive as this idea is, it tends to a belief that has been condemned by the Church: Arianism, named for its advocate Arius (d. 336). Arianism is defined as, "The main heresy which denied the full Divinity of Christ."[6] According to the Council of Nicea, Christ is fully human and fully divine, having both the attributes of a mortal and those of God. Therefore our worship, and each item of liturgy in our services, must address

---

6. *Concise Oxford Dictionary of the Christian Church*, 2nd rev. ed., s.v. "Arianism."

The God of Abraham, Isaac, and Jacob

both these attributes. Words that do not address the divine are relatively easy to identify. Music, ineffable, is harder to evaluate. However, if it sounds like a secular love song or a silly, comedic song, or carries no majesty, it may be devoid of the transcendent, holy character of the Godhead and hence denies or at least ignores the divine character of Christ and tends to the Arian heresy.

Practices and characteristics that signal possible Arianism occur when we:

1. Use words and music whose compositional and performance style derive from the world and ignore the holiness of Christ or God.
2. Offer music and words that characterize Jesus or God solely or principally as our friend, buddy, or co-laborer.
3. Present music or words whose sensual nature suggests that Jesus or God is our worldly lover.

EVALUATING HOLINESS IN MUSIC

Precisely defining character in music may be impossible, for character is to some extent ineffable and the Spirit will manifest itself in virtually unlimited ways. This does not mean, as some apparently believe, that every tune or musical style that appears is worthy for worship. How then do we make decisions, for God does enjoin us to "keep the Sabbath holy"? The possible abuses listed above provide some guidelines. Below, following supporting quotes, I translate these into the form of questions I would ask about a piece of music, or any liturgical item, before including it in worship. The answer to some of these questions is subjective and dependent on the particular congregation and circumstances.

John the Elder

> Beloved, do not believe every spirit, but test the spirits to see whether they are from God; for many false prophets have gone out into the world. By this you know the Spirit of God: every spirit that confesses that Jesus Christ has come in the flesh is from God, and every spirit that does not confess Jesus is not from God. And this is the spirit of the antichrist, of which you have heard that it is coming; and now it is already in the world. Little children, you are from God, and have conquered them; for the one who is in you is greater than the one who is in the world. They are from the world; therefore what they say is from the world, and the world listens to them. We are from God. Whoever knows God listens to us, and whoever is not from God does not listen to us. From this we know the spirit of truth and the spirit of error. (1 John 4:1–6)

Consider this excerpt from Theodore Runyon's *The New Creation: John Wesley's Theology Today*:

> Thus faith experience . . . is not threatened by this rational process of "testing the spirits" to see "whether they are of God" (1 John 4). Genuine faith welcomes this testing, for it desires to have demonstrated its continuity with historical Christianity even though, in each generation, the issues and problems that are current will lead to new and creative expressions of faith.[7]

---

7. Runyon, *New Creation*, 164.

The God of Abraham, Isaac, and Jacob

Questions Toward Discerning Character in Music

1. Is it purposed to and does it directly address the worship of God? If its purpose is otherwise, no matter how worthy, it is not for worship, but may be important to another church ministry.

2. Does its underlying theory and style of composition relate more closely to popular music than sacred? There certainly are examples where secular elements are artfully used for specific purposes, but this is in general a red flag that may point to idolatry.

3. Are the words and music designed to evoke an emotional effect? While emotion is not antithetical to worship, the use of cloying texts and tunes with cheap emotional hooks deny the transcendent awe appropriate to God.

4. Does its ideal performance depend on trappings from the secular world? Costumes, lights, speakers, choreography, and taped accompaniments in general point to the world.

5. Do the words and music honor both the humanity and divinity of Christ? If they relate only to the humanity, as in friend, buddy, or lover, they risk losing sight of or denying the divinity of Christ.

6. Do the words and music suggest a sensual relationship with Christ? Is it essentially a secular, sensual love song with the occasional mention of Christ or God? This tends toward the "lascivious songs" and "erotic rantings" proscribed by Chrysostom and Luther cited above.

7. Is the performance style designed more for effect than confession, reflection, communion, or adoration?

Holiness in Music

This suggests that the music serves the vanity of the performer or the manipulation of the congregation rather than the worship of God.

8. Does its character derive from a style of worship that the church at large or in particular has evolved beyond? As faith deepens the character of music for the church at large and congregations in particular matures over time, and thus some songs and musical styles are appropriately outgrown. "When I became an adult, I gave up childish ways" (1 Cor 13:11).

9. If the style and character of new songs are within traditionally accepted parameters, does it offer anything original, inspiring, challenging, fresh—that is to say, prophetic? It is not enough merely to be acceptable, it must break new ground musically and, if non scriptural, textually.

10. No matter how simple or complex, does the text benefit from the ancient and evolving arts of poetics, theology, and rhetoric? The text must spring from the tradition and show the sacrifice of comprehension and hard work in its construction.

11. Does the music benefit from the ancient and evolving character of musical arts? The music likewise must show the sacrifice of mastery of the tradition and the hard work of composition.

12. Is it an honest offering of our true selves? For example, using prerecorded accompaniments, except where other accompaniments are impossible, have us pretending to be something we are not. No matter how simple the offering, it is always better to offer ourselves honestly in worship.

The God of Abraham, Isaac, and Jacob

Both the positive and negative sides of these questions can be practiced with all styles of music. The Reformation was in part about music deemed to be too secular and ostentatious. Some felt that even Bach cantatas were too opulent for worship. Certainly there are humble, beautiful examples of contemporary music that are sung with devotion. My goal is to encourage the principle of discernment rather than provide a laundry list of proscribed pieces and musical styles. Style, however, as I state elsewhere, does carry theological meaning whose appropriateness should be weighed.

These criteria are not intended to condemn worthy secular activity and wholesome pleasures—an important part of the God-given life. Great secular music, entertainment, and activity are important and comprise necessary and salutary means of human expression. Personally, I enjoy many styles of secular music, and even perform folk music addressing a wide spectrum of human activity. The error lies in assuming that all good things belong in worship. Not all good things are holy. Including such non-worship items makes worship feel just like the world, breaking God's command to keep the Sabbath holy.

> Its priests have done violence to my teaching and have profaned my holy things; they have made no distinction between the holy and the common, neither have they taught the difference between the unclean and the clean, and they have disregarded my sabbaths, so that I am profaned among them. (Ezek 22:26)

Discerning true worship from idolatry is a delicate, profound, and timeless pursuit. The light of discernment is so frail at this juncture that, for example, the same piece of music can be idolatrous in one church and holy in another. This dialectic is true even in the same congregation, where

Holiness in Music

particular circumstances might call for a selection that would ordinarily not be appropriate in the congregation's worship life.

When we use inappropriate music for the wrong reasons, we may find the intended worldly gain; but it will inevitably amount to a noisy gong and clanging cymbal, or worse, will result in serving the powers and principalities. To hedge against this, we test the spirits of our selections to see if they address the God of Abraham, Isaac, and Jacob. True worship, though never its principal aim, will often bring worldly blessings, but will more importantly certainly bring the invaluable reward of communion with God.

5

Church Music Midrash

Chenaniah, leader of the Levites in music, was to direct the music, for he understood it. (1 Chr 15:22)

Church Music Midrash

VIRTUALLY ALL MAJOR CHRISTIAN denominations require their clergy to be deeply schooled in their distinct theological, sacramental, political, and exegetical traditions. The exegetical tradition is based on the Hebrew midrashic tradition, where interpretation of scripture begins with ideas generated and synthesized through generations of scholars, proceeding from the beginning of the Hebrew religion.

Like clergy and scholars schooled in the historic and evolving theology of the church, trained church musicians recognize and speak the hermeneutics (interpretative framework) of Western church music. And just as responsible pastor-theologians make certain that their church's liturgy adheres to agreed-upon theological church tenets, so all music presented in worship should commend itself to the musical canon of the church as authorized through this midrashic tradition. Thus, these musicians compose and select music that proceeds from this hermeneutic dialogue, and thereby hope to address the God of Abraham, Isaac, and Jacob.

Many ancient and some contemporary cultures have shamans—persons deemed to have extraordinary access to God, who use music, among other arts, to effect human-divine communion. These ancient skills, techniques, and repertories are passed from master to apprentice and have thus proceeded through the centuries. This is similar to the rabbinic midrashic tradition and the priestly clerical and musical tradition of the Jewish temple priests. In the Christian church, these talents and responsibilities have been inherited in part by the pastor and in part by the musician. Some divine truths and arts are discernible and expressible only through music. These are embodied and conveyed in the techniques, literature, and rituals of the art of music, but also signally in the sacred passing of the mantle from master to apprentice. Thus, the ancient musical arts have continued through the evolution of Western classical music. These musicians are charged with interpreting and disseminating the will of God as manifest in music.

While in graduate school I had the privilege of studying one summer at Cambridge with the late Peter LeHuray. Though I was there principally to learn of music and the English Reformation, for which he is renowned as a musicologist, he also taught me something of counterpoint and literature. He introduced me to some pieces, which he said, "make a fine effect." Among them were William Harris's (1883–1973) "Faire is the Heaven," a musical-theological *tour de force*, "See, See the Word is Incarnate," a stunningly original sacred work, and the eminently practical and holy anthem, "Almighty and Everlasting God," both by Orlando Gibbons (1583–1625).

I have used the first once in concert, the second several times in concert and worship, and the third many times in worship. I use these for the inherent nobility of the music; to discover the truths that, because of his recommendation, I know must be there; and to honor the trust he showed in commending the performance of these works, precious to the English tradition, to me. By studying with him, after the old British model of "reading" with him one on one, by spending time with him, meeting his family, and working hard to master the tasks he gave me, though it was but for a few short, though intense, weeks, I learned something of his character as a man and a church musician. Thus, though we never thought of it in these terms, he inducted me into the midrash of church musicians and gave me some skills by which I could carry this on when I returned to my work in the United States.

LeHuray was himself a product of Cambridge, where he studied with the eminent musicologist-performer

Church Music Midrash

Thurston Dart, who likewise had studied with a master and so forth, backward though time, the mentor-genealogy proceeds. *While my study with Peter LeHuray was too brief to claim this descent, the example illustrates the principle whereby the musical midrash is nurtured and entrusted from ancient forebears to each succeeding generation.*

Of course, learning and practicing this midrash is not dependent on studying at Cambridge. My first post out of college was at Park Road Baptist Church of Charlotte, North Carolina. Then it was a medium-sized church of about 700 members—larger and with a stronger music and worship program than I was ready to handle at so tender an age. After a couple of months, I got into serious trouble programming music that was too ambitious for the congregation and too difficult for the choir to learn in the time we had. The pastor and leaders of the congregation talked with me about the problems. Rather than firing me as I may have deserved, after my initial rush of vain indignation, they generously offered to have their finest singer and president of the choir, Claire Ashcraft, help me select music. She, gracious and wise and, though degreed in music, without presumption or overbearance, helped me select music for the next several months. As I recall, I accepted her advice in every instance, and over the period of this apprenticeship, as I learned to fly solo, we became lifelong friends. Thus she and a forbearing church taught a young overwrought college kid something about the realities of literature selection in a worshiping congregation and some of the wisdom and skill required to lead people.

The midrash, of course, applies to more than the selection of anthems, and is relevant to musical practices in parishes of all sizes. In the same church, the pastor, Charlie Milford, had gone through the entire Baptist hymnal and, with a committee of congregants, selected all the hymns

The God of Abraham, Isaac, and Jacob

they felt were theologically and musically appropriate for their use in worship. This was done shortly before my arrival; but as the selection of hymns was in my purview, over the six years of my tenure, I comprehended their selection list and also learned something of the criteria they used for selection. I also learned that not every hymn in the hymnal was appropriate for every congregation.

These shaman-mentors, LeHuray, Ashcraft, and Milford—and there are many more—taught me not only specific anthems and hymns that they believed were appropriate for worshiping the God of Abraham, Isaac, and Jacob, but also, thereby they trained me in the discernment of the appropriate character of music for worship; and not only these, they taught me that, before introducing music to worship, it was critical to subject it to this discernment—to "test their spirits." As Charlie Milford was fond of saying: "worship requires defense."

One way of testing the spirits is to learn the genealogy of music being considered for worship. Did its genesis derive from the midrash? Does its musical style grow out of antecedents in the music canon? Was it introduced by mentors who were themselves bred in the church's musical midrash? Certainly worthy worship music can spring from sources outside of the midrash, but this is nevertheless a strong place to begin discernment.

Thus we are taught and brought into the parlance of church musicians by our elders in the craft, but even after we become practicing professionals, we depend on our peers for advice, skills, and recommendations of literature. We meet for lunch, or call and ask what anthems colleagues are doing for Christ the King Sunday, or share that we have a fine youth soloist that we want to use on Palm Sunday—asking if they have a good piece for that combination. Or we might call and say we've heard John Smith's "Kyrie" is a

Church Music Midrash

fine piece. Have they done it? Is it hard? We may get a yes, or that it's awful, or that it works in a pinch, or it requires strong tenors, or it's a little flashy but the congregation will love it, or that it's only appropriate for stewardship Sunday or the like.

More formally, church musicians go to workshops and reading sessions where an accomplished church musician will share techniques and a list of anthems that she or he finds particularly good and useful. I have found many in such settings, including one of my favorites, "Surely, He Hath Borne Our Griefs" by Evan Copley, in a reading session led by the eminent choral conductor Ann Howard Jones.

Or more formally yet, we observe the performances and recordings of great conductors like the late Robert Shaw, and, while much of the literature he performed may be beyond the reach of some church choirs and congregations, his uncompromising rigor in the selection of literature and in performance excellence, though our resources and talents be ever so humble, nevertheless should inform our selections and challenge our standards.

Through their search for the best pieces for worship, by rehearsing, performing in worship, and observing their efficacy with choir, instrumentalists, and congregations, church musicians ferret out musical weaknesses and vanities; over decades and centuries, they hone the repertory, dropping pieces that don't measure up, and adding those that do. Some pieces, though perhaps making an initial splash, gradually fall out of use; while, over time and generations, those that have a sterling character eventually find their way into the permanent repertoire, and the repertoire itself becomes more and more refined, gradually evolving to more truly approach the character of Christ. Thus, in the holy sphere of worship and under the inspiration and providence of the Holy Spirit, musicians have shepherded a musical tradition that advances human-divine communion.

Church musicians at all levels of education and experience, though not formally, nor necessarily with their conscious knowledge, carry on this midrashic tradition of sacred music, contributing new techniques and forms to the church midrash and adding new works to the repertoire of works that they have found to be most efficacious for worship; thus they have created and maintain a church music canon.

> I will incline my ear to a proverb; I will solve my riddle to the music of the harp. (Ps 49:4)

During the medieval period composers were most often anonymous, but this evolution becomes more traceable in the development of counterpoint (the art of combining more than one musical line) through the schools of Notre Dame, the Burgundians, the Netherlands, Italy, Germany, and England. From the Baroque period, Western music moved substantively into the secular world and the path dissipates, but yet extant sacred lineaments nevertheless reveal how the tradition advances.

More or less consciously, church musicians perceive the centuries' old tradition, and based on this, chart a musical course into the future. The content of this repertory evolves as musicians interact with contemporary culture and God. Historically, the inclusion of music from secular sources was ideally accomplished by experts bred and trained in the musical and theological midrash of the church. Much is made of Martin Luther's use of secular tunes or even J. S. Bach's. In both cases, their relatively rare use of these was effected with care for their propriety for worship, and only after they had made adjustments sanctifying them for worship. (Contrast this with the relatively indiscriminate inclusion of secular styled music by some today.) Thus the musical canon is constantly evolving to include elements of secular culture, as it always has in the past, but ideally only as refined and authorized via the midrash.

Parish musicians whether self-aware or not, are prophets who know or are learning the ancient ritual songs and, on this basis and through this developing canon, guide their congregations toward God. Even where musicians are not formally trained, their congregation's call invokes a sacred responsibility and sanction of the Holy Spirit, guiding the musician's choices. No matter if church musicians fully comprehend the secrets or the power of what they play and sing—this is not for mortals to fully comprehend—they nevertheless respect, defend, share, and profess the ongoing tradition. Striving to address the God of Abraham, Isaac, and Jacob, they thus vouchsafe God's sacred songs to posterity.

6

Church Music Canon

Your statutes have been my songs wherever I make my home. (Ps 119:54)

Church Music Canon

THE HOLY SCRIPTURES ARE words given to humans by God that evolved over time in dialectic relation among God and humans, were written down and later codified by humans schooled in the prophetic tradition, and later still were collected as "the Word of God" for Jewish and Christian communities. The Christian scriptural canon has been set in its present form since the early fourth century. This was accomplished via an evolutionary process that allowed texts found to be authentically the Word of God to emerge from those found not to be. As newly discovered ancient documents come forward, this canon is subject to further interpretation. For example, Princeton Christian historian Elaine Pagels wrote: "What is clear is that the Gospel of Judas has joined the other spectacular discoveries that are exploding the myth of a monolithic Christianity and showing how diverse and fascinating the early Christian movement really was."[1]

My point here is not to bring light on the evolution of the Bible, about which I know little, but to show that the canon of scripture is a mutual enterprise between God and humanity. This does not, in my view, diminish, but rather increases its authority, value, and holiness, for it acknowledges the immanence of God in humanity, is born of our common journey, and underscores our responsibility as disciples for realizing God's word on earth.

If humanity can produce a canon of scripture inspired of God, then it can do so through other media as well, for God's communication to humanity is not limited to the spoken and written word. God communicates via all the senses and even in subconscious ways. While we may feel the strength and divine verity of these communications, their meanings often elude articulation. Doubtless, God

---

1. Pagels, "Gospel Truth."

The God of Abraham, Isaac, and Jacob

created the arts to explore and express matters beyond the reach of words. Had we the means to translate them cognitively, these artistic legacies could be evaluated and canonized as well.

Music, along with other arts, has ineffable spiritual characteristics, but also identifiable physical characteristics that are subject to evaluation. Thus theoretical analysis can be used to illumine meaning in music as well as soundness of compositional structure. Outside of obvious amateurisms—unfortunately too prevalent in some modern music—this is not easily done definitively, for who could conform, for example, Stravinsky to the harmonic tenets of the early twentieth century? Yet some of his sacred music is now justifiably part of the canon of Western Christian music.

The ineffability of music is perhaps why I have never seen a convincing analytical rationale prescribing a formula for precisely defining character in music. Robert Shaw touched on this when he compared the principles of musical composition to the construction of sound buildings—music is also dependent on quality of thought, materials, and construction.[2] I pose questions in chapter 4 that indirectly address the question.

While theoretical analysis can inform theological and musical character, the principal criteria for judging a composition's worth should be a more subjective sense of vitality, historical authenticity, character, and holiness, which particular music inspires consistently over time. Evaluating previously composed pieces that have earned this distinction and thus tacitly have joined the church music canon, one will inevitably find sound theoretical principles in their composition. I expect these criteria also figured materially in the selection of the scriptural canon.

2. Shaw, "Worship and the Arts," 375.

Church Music Canon

"And the Word became flesh and dwelt among us" (John 1:14). The Word then comprises not only the spoken and later written words of scripture, but also the holy truths carried in the liturgical arts that evolved with them, including music. It is the character of God carried in these media—John's logos—that became manifest in the flesh, incarnate in Jesus, that we strive to address, reveal, and instill in the souls of our fellow worshipers.

A lack of respect for the ancient tradition of music in the church is, in my view, a prime reason for today's effusion of pop culture music and the rampant marginalization of character in music for worship. *The acknowledgement of a canonic repertory in church music, similar to that in scripture, would increase the respect for music among church leaders and laity, and thus necessarily work improvement.*

EVOLVING MUSICAL CANON

The earliest Christian music derived from chant and song from synagogue and Greek worship. As the church spread through the Western world, it absorbed liturgy and music from subsumed religions and cultures. The monumental liturgy of the medieval Catholic Church—nearly all of which was sung—developed over centuries. It was codified into a minutely organized matrix of sung prayer, so subtle and rich as to have distinct songs for various parts of liturgies, for designated prayer times of each day of an annual cycle. This liturgy, springing from a disciplined, inspired, and timeless conversation with God, whose breadth, meaning, and reach surpass human ken, is among the greatest of human-divine achievements.

From the early days of the church, musicians began to improvise around the unison chant melodies commonly sung, and harmony gradually developed. When their improvisations ventured far enough away from the chant—and they wanted to reproduce what they had done—they invented notation. The notation allowed further experimentation, and composers started to add voices of increasing independence around the preexistent chant line, thus beginning polyphony (more than one tone). In early development, the chant line predominated as a relatively slow-moving foundation around which the other voices gravitated. By the Renaissance, the slow-moving *cantus firmus* (chant melody) was often dropped, and the other voices reached parity. The *cantus firmus* was carried in the independent voices, or, less obviously, the chant was not directly quoted but was absorbed into the very character of the voices themselves. Thus composers infused their new creations with the essence, if not the substance of the original chant; and via the work of subsequent composers, the spirit of the original chant repertory lives on.

Through subsequent centuries to the present day, Western church music has advanced this principle of history-honoring innovation. Works in the church music canon, though representing a wide range of styles, show their heritage from the music of previous periods—with Duruflé directly quoting chant at one end of the spectrum and Stravinsky representing another.

Though the compositional styles of Duruflé and Stravinsky could not have been predicted in advance, analysis of their works nevertheless illumines their descent from historical models. These composers' command of inherited compositional technique and their creative genius enabled them to combine the old in unprecedented ways and thereby to expand the compositional palette, thus magnifying the range of musical-liturgical expression for themselves and their followers. Somewhat like a child who grows to maturity and sets out into the world, Western music develops freely, but ever evolves from its roots—the canonic repertory of the church.

This canon is multidimensional, so that while proceeding in unity with the Holy Spirit, it nevertheless has subsets for each Christian tradition, from denominations down to individual congregations. It is broad enough to embrace many worship traditions and churches of all sizes. It is articulated through many musical performance styles, including the improvisatory. It accommodates churches with very formal, perhaps professional music programs, and those with informal worship traditions, with perhaps an all volunteer, or even no music staff. The literature ranges from the most difficult classical anthems to the simplest hymn, folk hymn, or spiritual. *The canon is not about the complexity or difficulty of the music presented, but about the character of the literature and its fidelity to the worship traditions of our forebears—the musical midrash.* There is a portion of the canon appropriate for and available to every Christian church.

DIVINE-HUMAN MUSICAL LANGUAGE

The body of Western chant evolved to be recognizably Christian, distinct in repertory and style from those of every other culture and religion—which have their own unique and invaluable repertories. It is truly a musical language with a common, recognizable ethos springing of communion with God. It is inclusive and evolutionary—for new styles and forms have been absorbed throughout history from many disparate cultures, and continue to be so today. Considering that it is built on Jewish and Greek sources, this musical divine-human conversation extends back to the dawn of humanity. With ears to hear, the ancient divine strains can be heard through the centuries in the tones of modern church music, and reach limitlessly through the future in an ever-expanding musical telos.

This evolution took place in dialogue with and sanction from God within the precincts of divine worship, thereby creating a divine-human musical language. This musical language is unique to the worship of God and, though drawing elements from, is distinct from secular culture.

A quintessential example of the integrality of music and prophecy is found in David: king, prophet, musician. He lived, warred, reigned and prayed in a constant musical dialogue with God. We have the words he composed or that were collected in his name in the Psalter. While not identifiably extant, this very music has nevertheless continued to be sung over the centuries; for this body of tunes, or the essence of their character, was conveyed through oral tradition to the early church and thence into Gregorian chant and modern sacred music and yet sings within the musical tradition. The Psalter is one important example of scripture, and there are others whose original music, though anonymous, yet lives in this musical tradition. *Music, thereby, shares with scripture a canonical role in conveying the ancient story of Christian religious heritage and prophetic truth.*

7

Pastoral Leadership

And every work that he undertook in the service of the house of God, and in accordance with the law and the commandments, to seek his God, he did with all his heart; and he prospered. (2 Chr 31:21)

The God of Abraham, Isaac, and Jacob

My principal professor at Yale, the late Richard F. French, more than anyone else in my life, impressed me with and gave me skills to address the sacred duty owed church music. He once said to me, "Your best is really okay." Abashed that he had not said that my best was "brilliant" or "unparalleled," I protested, "My best is okay?" "Yes," he said, "Your best is really okay." Given Mr. French's standards, this was indeed a strong compliment.

We are called to do our best. This may not make us geniuses, but it is enough—it is okay. Doing our best is prophetic. It affects us as individuals because it clarifies for us to what we are committed—in this case, to music and other liturgical arts in the service of worship. This inspires us to greater discipline and accomplishment in the service of worship, and makes us happier. We all feel better when we know we have done our best.

Often I observe in others and myself that when projects are sloughed off, the results, if not abject failure, lack the vitality for positive impact. No matter the talent and past accomplishment of the leader, uncommitted work falls flat—like a noisy gong or a clanging cymbal. On the other hand, I have witnessed many times, when individual or corporate best is given, success is often achieved with even inadequate talent or resources. Creation makes way for our best efforts. God blesses and magnifies our best efforts.

The minister (lay or clergy) truly called will ever strive to bring the people closer to God and into harmony with the will of God. This requires commitment and hard work. The lack of these, in my view, is the reason for the current malaise in the church and the crisis in worship. The discipline requisite to preach or to conduct music over and over, week in and week out, year in and year out, with acuity, creativity, and spirit-filled enthusiasm is daunting, and lamentably, all too rarely maintained.

Pastoral Leadership

His yoke is easy . . . (Matt 11:30). Such a discipline, while seemingly difficult, is in reality the easiest path. Habits of hard work begun in youth, college, seminary, and conservatory will have life-long benefits. As the student looks toward a lifetime of apparent cold, lonely, disciplined work, the prospect may seem over-daunting; but many of the rewards are unseen. As the regimen progresses, it comes easier, and more progress is made in less time; and moreover, as one moves through life, some of the process becomes innate and some of the virtues of discipline, provided the commitment remains, come without the work. It is a mystery.

True pastoral leadership emerges via a subtle dialectic between the authenticity and strength of vision of the leader, and the gift of loyalty from the congregation. In my view, this gift from the congregation has to be earned through devotion, sacrifice, and fidelity. The congregation needs to know that the leader loves them and is working for their best interest. Thus, even if they should not like a particular decision, their respect will endure. God will provide the sincere leader the right opportunity to show love for the congregation.

Leaders will love the people enough not merely to care for their needs, but enough, even when against their expressed wishes, to pull them toward the will of God. Every suggestion from congregants, however, will be received as an offering. Whether or not the suggestion is followed, it will enter the leader's memory and will more or less consciously play a part of the subtle matrix of ministry. In my experience, if the suggestion is seriously and sincerely intended, often an opportunity will present itself for it to be employed, even where it results in a liturgical item unusual for the worshiping body. This is among the ways the Holy Spirit inspires prophecy from the people. The leader, considering (praying) over the tradition of the church, and her or his love for the congregant, has eyes to see the prophetic opportunity when God presents it. These opportunities sometimes bring radically creative acts to our worship.

Conversely, one does, however, through the insight and strength of prayer, need to say no when no is the right answer. Where done sincerely, this strengthens the spiritual depth of the service and ultimately builds respect for the leader. Worship must be defended from the relentless encroachments of the world.

Consider the following scenario. A youth Sunday school teacher of long-standing popularity decided to take a leave. Youth leaders found a replacement that appeared to be qualified, but, though well meaning, did not have that *je ne sais quoi* that appealed to these particular youth, and attendance dropped dramatically. To address this, youth leaders brought in a band to perform secular styled music in tandem with the youth program. This, they proposed, would bring the youth back. I don't know to what lengths the leaders had gone in finding a teacher who possessed characteristics auguring for success. My guess is that they, without much discernment, happily took the first volunteer; and, while the problems with the youth's interest in the teacher were generally acknowledged, rather than address these, either by helping or replacing the teacher, they brought in a band.

This, on a larger scale, is exactly what happens in the worship practice of many churches. Facing dwindling numbers, rather than addressing problems with their ministries or staff, they bring in bands as the panacea for meeting number and budget goals. Many welcome this apparent solution to their institutional problems without considering whether the new music or texts are faithful to their theology, or without recognizing the dire break this entails

Pastoral Leadership

with the musical and liturgical traditions of their forebears. In these instances, bringing in the band covers up the real problems with the church and uses the music of the world to tempt the faithful away from the tried and true. In some instances church leaders claim their previously used forms of worship and education are no longer valid, when it is not the forms, but poor execution that is to blame.

In the scenario I cite above, the youth leaders should have fixed the problem with Sunday school rather than covering it up with a band. Similarly, all churches should ensure that their leaders and ministries are faithful, vital, and compelling. For solutions to problems, we should look to the wisdom of our forebears and not to the false promises of the world. As Peter says, "Discipline yourselves; keep alert. Like a roaring lion your adversary the devil prowls around, looking for someone to devour" (1 Pet 5:8).

Those who strive to keep the language of music and worship holy will have to stand down the powers and principalities. Not only will the world resist, but as Moses in the desert had to conquer the dangers from without as well as his own peoples' infidelity to God, so we must overcome our church's infatuation with the world. For this, as Jesus said to his disciples, one must "be wise as serpents and innocent as doves" (Matt 10:16).

Pandering to the people, always playing it safe, will make some people happy in the short run, and will allow the leader to parade in hero's clothing—temporarily. This course, however, will always result in long-term unhappiness, and ensures at last a fatal contempt for the leader. Effective ministry requires taking considered risks and holding out for long-term truth against the tide of short-term fancy. Powers and principalities flourish in teasing slights toward quick salvation. Moving quickly and using

The God of Abraham, Isaac, and Jacob

foul means, they make promises that vanish into the dark of despair.

> *Broad is the road that leads to death,*
> *and thousands walk together there,*
> *but wisdom shows a narrow path,*
> *with here and there a traveler.*[1]

How do we know that God has called us to try something new, like a piece of music that may not be in the canonic repertory I discussed earlier? We consider how it comes to us. Does it come naturally from trusted folk in the congregation? Does it have an authentic place in some special liturgical observance? Often, I have included such non-traditional music in extraordinary circumstances, answering what I believed to be the prophetic voice. Having done it once however, does not mean we have to keep doing it. A common error is to repeat a liturgical item whose novelty made it appropriate once. Unless it is a masterpiece, rarely does the repetition of such an event have the same prophetic impact. In this case, it's better to have done the item only once and leave the valuable memory intact and distinct.

For the right pastoral-prophetic reasons, making exceptions in the stylistic mores of a congregation is important. Once leaders have proven their mettle in maintaining discipline, the occasional change does not threaten the strength of the tradition or the holy character of a congregation's worship.

The leader has to do the right thing in every situation. Doing the wrong thing, even for a short-term good, will always bring discontinuity and the judgment of God, though this will always be in God's way and time. How is the right thing determined? Certainty is elusive, but thoughtful

---

1. Watts, "Broad is the Road," 38.

Pastoral Leadership

decisions based on knowledge of the congregation's faith tradition, arrived at through prayer, sacrifice, and love offer our best chance of success. As Yale Chaplain Vannorsdall once said, "When we fail, we may fully enjoy the grace God will provide when we know we have done our best."

God's truth, however, is immutable and proceeds with providential strength. The call to stand against the force of popular tide will come to every true minister, often in the minor decisions of week-to-week ministry, and rarely, if ever, in risking one's professional life. To the committed minister, these challenges are part of the prophetic life.

When I came to my current post twenty-seven years ago, I began to press our congregation to sing Advent hymns during Advent. In my experience most protestant churches sing Christmas carols from the first Sunday of Advent through Christmas. The reasoning goes that everyone loves Christmas carols—no one more than I; the culture is playing them and we can't beat the culture, and we only meet on Sundays and don't have enough opportunity to sing them otherwise. My argument has been that we lose the beauty and theological potency of the carols when we sing them prematurely and that, more importantly, we lose the prophetic power of Advent by moving directly to Christmas—naming the season Advent, but offering the sermons and music of Christmas, does not Advent make. *This plays into the powers by succumbing to the cultural temptation of celebrating without the sacrifice required to merit it.* Our prophetic tradition is about overcoming cultural temptations. We must prepare the way for Christ. When we have undertaken the sacrifice of Advent, we release the inherent power of Christmas carols and may truly enjoy and reap the spiritual benefits of the gift of Christ.

I am grateful to acknowledge that our congregation has evolved to singing Advent hymns and offering Advent

The God of Abraham, Isaac, and Jacob

music through most of the season. Though I have never been solely in charge of hymn selection, I nevertheless carry the blame for depriving the congregation of singing Christmas carols as they had been accustomed. I have striven to ameliorate this by offering a carol sing close to Christmas. In my view, I have loved our people enough to forego something popular for something they will value even more. Nevertheless I have dubbed myself the "Grinch Who Stole Christmas"!

In a recent Advent season I received an unexpected gift. A congregant had left our communion for personal reasons about a year earlier; and, as I heard, was worshiping at a mega church that used popular-styled music. I was surprised and honored to hear from her recently that she now understood why and was grateful that I did not encourage Christmas carols during Advent. I receive this as a gift of the Magi, and take it as a small affirmation of holding out for long-term spiritual gain at the cost of short-term popularity.

From the previous chapters, it might be inferred that one should not lead music in a church without a doctorate in music, liturgics, and theology. Not so. Each person is equally qualified in the eyes of God for the setting to which they are genuinely called. PhDs can draw on the knowledge God has led them to acquire, as those with no formal education do from their own experiences. Song leaders in rural parishes with a handful in the choir—or no choir, with perhaps no formal church music education—have their life's experience and that of their forebears to draw on. The African or Indian shaman, Catholic or Jewish cantor, Muslim Iman, Hindu and Buddhist Gurus, and Anglican organist-choirmaster, etc. all have their unique and worthy calling from God. There are prophets with no education and dilettantes with doctorates, and vice versa. It is not the particular position description of the particular faith's musicians or their individual qualifications that are paramount; but rather it is the principle of recognizing the tradition as holy, and then sharing, leading, and prophesying through sacrificial effort in the context of love of God and the people that inspires true worship. Liturgy in worship should be on a never-ending gradient upward. While never achieving perfection in any given service, we strive to do a little better every week. This is possible, regardless of our level of training, experience, or ability, if we offer God our very best.

> Not that I have already obtained this or have already reached the goal; but I press on to make it my own, because Christ Jesus has made me his own. Beloved, I do not consider that I have made it my own; but this one thing I do: forgetting what lies behind and straining forward to what lies ahead, I press on towards the goal for the prize of the heavenly call of God in Christ Jesus. (Phil 3:12–14)

8

Making Decisions

Honor your father and mother. (Exod 20:12)

Making Decisions

AMONG THE DIALECTICS OPERATIVE on the path to truth is that of divine directive versus immanence or, in human terms, hierarchical versus democratic leadership. Humans want strong leadership while simultaneously wanting freedom—congregants want and need prophetic leadership, but they also want what they enjoy in worship. Similarly, church leaders want to provide leadership informed by the church's tradition, but they also want their liturgies to appeal to their congregations.

There is danger and potential idolatry at the extremes of both ends of these principles. When the church makes an idol of tradition, it loses relevance and touch with the people; when it makes an idol of pleasing people, it loses touch with the church's heritage and with God. The give and take of this dialectic may be observed throughout the history of the church, the writings of church fathers and mothers, and in proceedings of church councils whose promulgations have strongly influenced the role of music in worship. It was evident in Moses' relations with the Israelites in the desert and figures prominently in the day-to-day business and liturgies of every contemporary church.

The great twentieth-century Baptist preacher Carlyle Marney once told a group of training pastors, "If you get out too far ahead of your congregation, they mistake you for the enemy and start shooting." Thus the prophetic tradition of the church must always take care that it remain integrally related to the people.

For the other side, I quote Jesus: "For those who want to save their life will lose it, and those who lose their life for my sake will save it" (Luke 9:24). Trying to please everyone—"saving your life"—will ultimately please no one. Everyone will wind up shooting at you, and you'll not have the shield of God's truth to protect you; thus, you will lose your spiritual life. This, in my view, is the source of

The God of Abraham, Isaac, and Jacob

the problem: all too often the church has strayed from its inherited theological-musical principles in a vain attempt to attract congregants in order to "save their lives." This has had the unintended effect of marginalizing the teachings of our historic church forebears—those who invested their lives, who comprehended the church's history and practice and, through their wisdom and spiritual strength, advanced to the highest levels of the church. Thus their needed influence on character in church liturgy has been weakened, putting us in danger of worshiping gods other than the God of Abraham, Isaac, and Jacob. (Please see quotes from church forebears in chapter 4.) When we do not follow the wisdom of these and other of our church forebears, we break the fourth commandment to honor our fathers and mothers.

The truths we inherit from our forebears sometimes seem unattractive, too demanding to follow. Too often we have jettisoned them, rather than discerning how they can be vitalized for a worship that has authority and prophecy. Our very civilization depends on the successive contributions of our forebears. This is true in all arenas of human endeavor, and everyone except the most abject nihilists, whether they know and admit it or not, benefits from this. So it is, or ought to be, in church music.

ADMINISTRATIVE CHALLENGE

A cardinal source of the break with tradition lies in the way decisions are made about music in the church. Virtually all churches are run by professional clergy. Though ideally in consultation with the congregation and the church hierarchy, the final decisions are most often made by the senior pastor. This is also true at the denominational level, where typically clergy make decisions on policy and set liturgical models. Certainly lay people participate, but in

Making Decisions

my denomination, United Methodist, polity is weighted heavily in favor of the pastor's authority in every area of the church's life.

While this works well in many cases, it presents the opportunity for conflict and error. In church music, it means that the pastor is ultimately in charge of an area for which he or she ordinarily has no education or training. I took classes and lived with seminarians at Yale and taught at Emory's Candler School of Theology for ten years. While both schools offer excellent theological instruction, seminarians nevertheless receive little to no education in music and precious little in liturgy for the Master of Divinity. This is true in most seminaries nationally. With a few exceptions, music and liturgy are considered ancillary to the core disciplines of Bible, exegesis, preaching, and pastoral care. Regarding denominational credentialing, candidates for ordination must endure grueling examinations to ensure orthodoxy of doctrine, theology, and polity, but what of the pastor's supervisory role in parish music? Granting that it is impossible for a seminarian to master all church disciplines in three years, the integrality of music and its potentially incendiary role in worship demand more attention. Thus seminary graduates go on to parishes where, as CEO, they, no matter how ill-prepared, have ultimate authority over the music in the church and over the parish musician as well. The musician who has devoted her or his life, who has been trained for and called to the divine art of church music, has therefore no ultimate authority on how it is practiced in the parish.

Samuel Sebastian Wesley, Charles Wesley's grandson, wrote in 1875 of his over forty years as a cathedral musician:

> I left London when very young for Hereford, intending to compose chiefly for the Church but ... there is not only no reward for this but, far

> worse, such efforts bring an artist of eminence into conflicts with the insufficient means for performing music at Cathedrals: this state of things is the natural result of such an anomaly as that of one professional calling being wholly supervised by another—viz., Musicians by Clergymen, with no other laws for order than those of Henry the Eighth's time and the common law which treats organists as the servants of the Clergy so that no recognition of the Musician as an Artist and gentleman has any place in a Court of Law.[1]

Of course there are many instances where the pastor is wise and respectful of all employees and their disciplines. I have been privileged to work with some great pastors, from whom I enjoyed respect and freedom, and learned much from their preaching, leadership, and wisdom. Also, we musicians sometimes have made matters worse by being mere performers rather than pastoral musicians and by showing ourselves to be unnecessarily defensive and uncooperative. Granting sins and the need for grace on many sides, there is nevertheless a systemic administrative problem that is productive of results dangerous to our faith.

There are important reasons why this problem is growing worse. Pastors are subjected to tremendous pressure to make their congregations grow and to bring in the requisite funds to support important ministries. They see some churches apparently booming by jettisoning their worship traditions and importing materials and traditions from popular culture. Many have followed this route. It is far easier to pander to popular tastes than to undergo the discipline requisite to follow the Word of God. It is far easier to hire musicians to put on a popular show than to

---

1. S. Wesley, introduction, xv.

Making Decisions

undertake the commitment and hard work requisite for vital ministry; the self-critical appraisal and infusion of energy and hard work into all ministries—including music—that is required to attract outsiders to genuine spirituality. No leaders would advise teenage children to forget their moral teaching and do whatever it takes to be popular, but many nevertheless advise their congregations to do the liturgical-musical equivalent.

This discipline needs to be manifest not just with individuals, as advised in chapter 7, but also in local churches and in the highest levels of denominational organization. Why, for example, do ministry and church music no longer have caché among the brightest and most able students as career options? Why are seminaries and universities producing so few strong preachers and church musicians? *The lack of demand for the best at the highest levels is a self-fulfilling prophecy of mediocrity.* Though usually unvoiced, this lack of critical commitment is sensed throughout church hierarchies, in congregations, and even in the unchurched culture, where people, often without perceiving why, are thereby not drawn to church. Disciplined commitment begets excellence and inspires attention, respect, and emulation.

ECCLESIAL TRADITION

While the practice varies widely from denomination to denomination and from church to church, every denomination and virtually every church and pastor would maintain that their liturgical practice is based on authorized and considered theological and ecclesial traditions. This is especially true of exegesis, preaching, prayers, and other verbal liturgical acts. Preachers vaunt their exegetical study as authority for the rhetoric of their sermons.

The God of Abraham, Isaac, and Jacob

In some instances, the same denominations, churches, and clergy, in startling contrast, practice no similar standards for other liturgical elements, and most notably, music. Church music has a history, a scholarly discourse, and an ecclesial tradition equal to that of theology, homiletics, and any other worship art. Some of the same people who demand fidelity to theological tenets will permit and even insist on music that has no relation to the tradition of the church. Given the nearly universally accepted importance of music in worship and its influence on congregants, this is tragic.

> They sacrificed to demons, not God, to deities they had never known, to new ones recently arrived, whom your ancestors had not feared. (Deut 32:17)

I once heard a prominent pastor-theologian, for whom I otherwise have great respect, say that his church had begun an evening contemporary worship service. He commented that they found a young theology student to be clergy for the service and found someone competent in contemporary music to lead the music. I bristled, for it appeared that they had found someone respectful of and at least learning the theological canon to lead the liturgy, but someone unschooled in the tradition of church music to lead the music. Whether or not my assumption on the musician's background is true in this instance, this certainly is the pattern employed by many churches throughout the United States. Theological traditions are considered inviolable, but theological-musical traditions are too often thought expendable. Thus the style and character of the music are thought to be of no importance. This practice violates the spirit of the following statement from the United Methodist Book of Discipline and doubtless similar tenets of other denominational traditions:

> Nonetheless, the basic measure of authenticity in doctrinal standards, whether formally established or received by tradition, has been their fidelity to the apostolic faith grounded in Scripture and evidenced in the life of the church through the ages.[2]

When we confess the Nicene Creed, we commit to the Apostolic Church and thus, not only to the Apostles of Christ, or to the succession of bishops, but also to the inherited traditions of the church which this succession represents. This is also the case in the Apostles Creed were we confess belief in the Holy Catholic (universal) Church—including the church's present and past.

Worship planners would never consider throwing out the Bible, yet many happily throw out the music to which much of scripture was sung and which has evolved along with scriptural interpretation through the centuries. Remember that the Psalter was the hymnbook of ancient Israel and that the rest of scripture is rife with the texts of song. Few would admit to throwing out the inherited exegetical tradition of the church—at least not to their seminary professors—but some are happy to throw out the equivalent in church music. They would be laughed out of their clergy assemblies for doing the former, and are too often applauded for the latter. Thus, many churches have turned their backs on their inherited musical and worship traditions, and offer music and liturgies drawn from and, knowingly or not, too often offered to the world.

> What do I imply then? That food sacrificed to idols is anything, or that an idol is anything? No, I imply that what pagans sacrifice, they sacrifice to demons and not to God. I do not want you to be partners with demons. You cannot drink

---

2. United Methodist Church, *Book of Discipline*, 42.

> the cup of the Lord and the cup of demons. You cannot partake of the table of the Lord and the table of demons. (1 Cor 10:19–21)

As a young man, full of hubris, I thought that if people have always been doing something one way, then there must be a better way; and I'm going to find and do it. Now that I am older, I think if folk have always been doing something one way, and I don't see the reason, then I'd better do it their way until I learn the reason. This way, not only will I learn something important, I'll have a chance of addressing the God of Abraham, Isaac, and Jacob, and withal, will be honoring my mothers and fathers.

9
Misconceptions

Set your mind on divine things. (Mark 8:33)

The God of Abraham, Isaac, and Jacob

Discerning the will of God and learning to follow divine rather than human ways is a constant and timeless journey, requiring us to be "wise as serpents and innocent as doves" (Matt 10:16) and to sacrifice apparent worldly security and gain to follow Christ. Jesus challenges his disciples and us to this journey.

> But turning and looking at his disciples, he rebuked Peter and said, "For you are setting your mind not on divine things but on human things." He called the crowd with his disciples, and said to them, "If any want to become my followers, let them deny themselves and take up their cross and follow me. For those who want to save their life will lose it, and those who lose their life for my sake, and for the sake of the gospel, will save it. For what will it profit them to gain the whole world and forfeit their life? Indeed, what can they give in return for their life? Those who are ashamed of me and of my words in this adulterous and sinful generation, of them the Son of Man will also be ashamed when he comes in the glory of his Father with the holy angels." (Mark 8:33–38)

During my forty years working as a church musician, I have heard many excuses for replacing music of character with poor quality music. Most of these are driven by a laudable desire to bring more people into the church—a goal we all share. Some were doubtless prompted by misuses of the art of music in specific instances. Others sound logical on the surface and thus have gained adherents. Some in various permutations, have been used throughout history and will doubtless reappear in the future. Below, I give examples along with my responses.

Misconceptions

JESUS WENT INTO THE WORLD AND MIXED WITH
SINNERS, DOESN'T THIS MEAN WE SHOULD USE
WORLDLY MUSIC IN OUR WORSHIP?

Jesus went into the world, but he never changed his character to match that of the world; rather, in every instance he transfigured the world into the realm of God. We also go into the world and invite the world into worship, but we do not change our worship to match the character of the world. Rather, we bring the world into the worship of God in the tradition of Abraham, Isaac, and Jacob.

WHY SHOULD THE DEVIL HAVE ALL THE
GOOD TUNES?

I've heard this question attributed to Martin Luther, Charles Wesley, and others. I'll leave the facts to the musicologists. People bring it up to justify introducing secular elements into the liturgy, especially music. Whatever use of secular tunes—for example, tunes originally used for love songs—Wesley, Luther, and other church leaders made was done very sparingly and after careful editing via their theological acumen and their highly developed churchly sensibilities, and in Luther's case, professional musical training. Luther did use the great tune often attributed to Samuel Scheidt for "Innsbruck ich muss dich lassen" as a hymn. The only example of which I am personally aware of a secular tune used by the Wesleys was the tune to Henry Purcell's "Fairest Isle, All Isle's Excelling" from his opera, *King Arthur*. Charles Wesley paraphrased John Dryden's words into his great hymn "Love Divine, All Loves Excelling," sung to Purcell's tune. The Wesleys thus borrowed a secular tune from one of the greatest composers in history. Contrast this to the apparent wholesale copying of secular music and styles

The God of Abraham, Isaac, and Jacob

by many contemporary churches, for which there is no justification in scripture or church history.

THE OLD WAYS ARE FAILING, LOOK AT THE NUMBERS.

We might as well say that our ancestors failed us or that God has failed. Scripture is the oldest of our recorded ways; should we throw scripture out too? Certainly we have to be constantly creative in ministry, but all too often the real problem is not the old ways but our poor execution that produces failure. It is not the old ways, but *we* who are failing our ancestors and God through sloth and heeding false promises of easy solutions offered by the world.

IT DOESN'T MATTER WHAT WE SING SO LONG AS PEOPLE LIKE IT.

Imagine Moses in the desert deferring to the popular wishes of the people over against the will of God, or Jesus telling the moneychangers in the temple, "proceed, by all means." While it seems self-evident that whatever attracts people to church is a good thing, the thrust of prophecy holds against the blandishments of popular society. Nowhere does the scripture say "if it feels good, do it;" "if people like it, then it's good;" "if you would know the will of God, look to popular culture"; or "go forth and copy the world." Few would admit to such, but this is all too often the de facto practice of some churches today. This puts the worldly pleasures of the people over the wishes of God—putting the god of Mammon over the God of our forebears. In worship, we should offer what we believe pleases God rather than what we believe pleases humanity.

Misconceptions

Here is a quote from John Wesley's preface to one of the Wesleyan hymnbooks, where he condemns the singing of poor quality hymns from another hymnbook despite their popularity. This same sentiment may be attributed to Calvin, Luther, and many other church leaders.

> First, out of those two hundred and thirty-two hymns, I have omitted seven and thirty. These I did not dare to palm upon the world; because fourteen of them appeared to me very flat and dull: fourteen more, mere prose, tagged with rhyme: and nine more to be grievous doggerel. But a friend tells me, "some of these, especially those two that are doggerel double distilled, namely, "The despised Nazarene," and that which begins, "A Christ I have, O what a Christ have I," are hugely admired, and continually echoed from Berwick-upon-Tweed to London." If they are, I am sorry for it: it will bring deep reproach on the judgment of the Methodists. But I dare not increase that reproach, by countenancing, in any degree, such an insult both on religion and common sense. And I earnestly intreat all our preachers, not only never to give them out, but to discountenance them by all prudent means, both in public and private.[1]

Thus Wesley did not care how many members or clergy liked the hymns; he adjured the clergy to denounce them. Thus their popularity held no sway with Wesley. Contrast this with the practice of many churches today, some even citing Wesley erroneously for authority, who apparently use some music principally for its popularity.

---

1. J. Wesley, *Pocket Hymn Book*, preface.

The God of Abraham, Isaac, and Jacob

> IT DOESN'T MATTER HOW YOU GET THERE, SO LONG AS THE END IS GOOD.

This is a false notion by which many historic ills have been perpetrated. Bad means lead to bad ends.

> SECULAR-STYLED MUSIC IS SO POPULAR. DON'T WE HAVE TO ADOPT IT?

Popularity does not prove verity. Sin is very popular, but not something we want to advance. Heresies were so popular with their adherents that the church had to formally condemn them. Popular worldly music certainly does merit the church's attention, provided their spirits are tested with concomitant censure or support.

> ISN'T SECULAR-STYLED MUSIC SAVING MANY CHURCHES?

Certainly saving churches is an important goal, but we need to understand what it is about churches we are trying to save. Our institutions? Our faith practice? We are obligated to see that it is Christ's church we are saving, not the church of Mammon. That an organization is growing numerically does not necessarily mean it is serving Christ. This is why scripture warns us of idolatry and false prophets. Growth is good, provided the spirits are tested.

> MUSIC HAS NO INHERENT CHARACTER APART FROM THE WORDS.

This is easily disproved by singing the words of "Amazing Grace" to the Gilligan's Island television show theme song,

Misconceptions

and considering the radically different affects of the melodies and profound change in the perception of meaning. Though impossible to precisely articulate, who can listen to Beethoven's fifth symphony, or Billy Strayhorn's "Take the A Train" and not apprehend meaning? Calvin, Luther, and other church forebears testified to the power of music distinct from the words. Calvin said that "[music] *has a secret and almost incredible power to move our souls in one way or another . . .* [when melody is added to the words] *it pierces the heart much more strongly and enters within; as wine is poured into the cask of a funnel.*"[2] The idea of music having no inherent character is specious, but it is used over and over again to justify the use of bad music in worship— "The words are sacred, so it must be good." Both music and words must be holy.

YOUNGER GENERATIONS, YOUTH, AND CHILDREN CAN'T RELATE TO THAT OLD MUSIC.

While well intended, this speaks from the idolatry of changing the style and content of worship to match the shifting sands of popular taste that I have addressed elsewhere.

William Ralph Inge (1860–1954), professor of Divinity at Cambridge and Dean of St. Paul's Cathedral said, "If you marry the spirit of your generation, you will be a widow in the next."[3]

> We have blown up balloons, danced in the aisles, marched behind banners; we have turned to jazz and we have sung ditties whose theological content makes a nursery rhyme sound like Thomas Aquinas. But it is not enough to make

2. Calvin, "Epistle to the Reader," 347.
3. Inge, *Diary of a Dean*, 12.

> things livelier, or set to music our aspirations and agendas. We can do better than that, and we must, for when the truth of God as made actual in Christ and attested in the gospel evokes the truthful praise of God, Christian worship enacts an alternative to the secularism which otherwise deludes us with its promises.[4]

Jesus said, "If you would save your life you will lose it" (Luke 9:24). Music drawn from or inspired of the church music canon, carefully chosen for the intended age group and ecclesial purpose, is even more engaging than music chosen for its worldly allure, and withal, more assuredly communicates the Gospel.

At least twice I have heard worship leaders say something like this: "We did a survey of our community, and found that only 10 percent listened to classical music. We decided we had no business forcing this old music onto people." My response has been, "When you found that only 5 percent of the people read the Bible, did you decide you had no business imposing that on them?" My point is not that classical music narrowly defined is the only music appropriate for worship, but that we do not discard our inherited worship forms, neither our scripture nor our music, to match the tastes of the world.

---

4. Keck, *Church Confident*, 42.

Misconceptions

UNCHURCHED FOLK CAN'T BEGIN WITH TRADITIONAL LITURGY AND MUSIC; WE HAVE TO USE THE MUSIC AND LITURGICAL STYLES OF CONTEMPORARY SECULAR EXPERIENCE. FROM THERE WE CAN LEAD THEM DEEPER INTO FAITH.

Consider the devil tempting Jesus in the desert. "I will give you the whole world if you would just . . . " The danger of this premise is made clear if one applies it to our children: "It's okay to bend your character so long as it's for a good cause." "It's okay to seduce someone to be your friend by dropping your standards so long as you ultimately gain their friendship." The very process introduces sin into the relationship and fouls the result.

Further, we are not permitted by God to dilute worship for worldly gain. We are certainly called to evangelize, but not to put other gods in place of the true God. Putting anything else, even the otherwise critical ministry of evangelism ahead of worship is idolatry. We authorize and strengthen evangelism when we put the worship of the God of Abraham, Isaac, and Jacob first.

This false premise also suggests that the worship of God as given by our forebears is not inherently winsome. Done in spirit and in truth, the worship of God is irresistible and will bring the world to it. "I was glad when they said to me, 'Let us go to the house of the Lord!'" (Ps 122:1). After Augustine—our souls, longing to rest with God, recognize true worship and are drawn to it.

The God of Abraham, Isaac, and Jacob

SHOULDN'T WE BE INCORPORATING ALL STYLES AND TRENDS OF WORLD CULTURES IN OUR WORSHIP? AFTER ALL, JESUS COMMANDS US TO TAKE THE GOSPEL INTO THE WORLD.

Yes—take the gospel, but not other gods or the "world" back into the world. It is a canard to say that each church has to use every style of worship and music to reach folk they are not already reaching. This reason has been used as an excuse to have the church follow trends and fads and to dilute the essential worship of the church. We do not surrender the character of Christ's church in order to be popular. Certainly good liturgy will be inclusive of world cultures, for the church welcomes all; but we do not remake the church into the image of the world.

CAN'T GOD SPEAK THROUGH ANY MUSIC, AND IN ANY TIME AND PLACE?

Of course, God can and does speak through all means, times, and places, but we, who are weak, ignorant, and sinful, need the guidance and form of the inherited human-divine language of worship in order to respond appropriately. The scripture admonishes us to offer an acceptable sacrifice, giving us the responsibility to test the spirits of what we offer.

WE CAN'T CENSURE THE MOVEMENT OF THE SPIRIT.

When the propriety of a popular liturgical item is challenged, this excuse often emerges. Certainly the Holy Spirit does lead us in new ways, but not every idea is of the Spirit.

Misconceptions

Again, John the Elder enjoins us to test the spirits (1 John 4:1–4).

It doesn't matter whether musicians are trained in the historic music of the church so long as they are competent and their hearts are in the right place.

Not all churches can afford professionally trained staff and, as mentioned earlier, training is not essential to church musicians or clergy who are truly called. But churches that can afford trained personnel often hire musicians untrained in the ancient history of music, when they would rarely consider hiring a preacher untrained in theology or church polity. Church music is a complex, subtle, and powerful art whose practice can do great good or harm. The more we know of its history and practice, the greater our chance of using it appropriately for the worship of God. Concerning music, Calvin says, "we must be the more careful not to abuse it, for fear of soiling and contaminating it, converting it to our condemnation when it was dedicated to our profit and welfare."[5]

Musicians are simply trying to put on musical displays to build their reputations.

There are musicians who do music for the wrong reasons and this should be discouraged. This can be true of practitioners of any style of music, or preaching, for that matter. Because doing good works advances the reputation of the musician does not make it bad, however; for it is impossible

---

5. Calvin, "Epistle to the Reader," 347.

The God of Abraham, Isaac, and Jacob

to do good works, however humbly, without advancing the doer's reputation. Good things are good for many reasons.

> SO-CALLED GREAT CHURCH MUSIC IS PROPAGATED BY MUSICAL ESTHETES WHO CARE ONLY ABOUT THEIR MUSIC AND NOTHING FOR THE PASTORAL LIFE OF THE CONGREGATION, MAKING AN IDOL OF CLASSICAL CHURCH MUSIC.

This statement is doubtless true for some musicians and a temptation for more. That there are some poor practitioners, however, does not make the tradition itself bad.

> TRADITIONAL MUSICIANS ARE JUST DEFENDING THEIR LIVELIHOODS.

A classically trained musician defending traditional music is de facto defending the profession. That fact does not discount the verity of the defense. Using this argument one would also have to discount the arguments of popular musicians and even the clergy who vaunt it as the way to save the church, for it appears to be in their self-interest.

> TRADITIONALISTS ARE JUST AFRAID OF CHANGE, WANTING TO WORSHIP THE SAME WAY THEY ALWAYS HAVE, MAKING AN IDOL OUT OF THEIR TRADITIONS.

Certainly there is sin in holding onto dead tradition. The materials and motives of the traditionalist should be weighed just as carefully as those of proponents of change. The tradition should be constantly evolving. But just

Misconceptions

because tradition is defended does not mean tradition is wrong.

A common rallying point for using secular-styled music is, that just as the Wesleys' hymnody was originally controversial but is now known to be good, this new controversial trend will be good as well. Granting that the Wesleys' hymnic innovations were provocative yet prophetic, it does not hold that everything that is controversial is therefore good. Most controversial innovations in the church's history have been found to be false and were left where they began.

Fidelity to the will of God has always required strong defense—witness the prophets. In virtually every arena of human endeavor, tradition is honored. This should be especially so in our most important endeavor, the worship of God.

It's only music—what's the big deal?

I have shared in several places the importance of music in worship attested to by church leaders. Calvin notes that "we find by experience that it [music] has a secret and almost incredible power to move our hearts in one way or another."[6]

Quality of the music for performance doesn't matter, so long as the performer's heart is in the right place.

I was once told by a pastor that he could prove that the quality of a performance was irrelevant, for at a conference he had heard a choir of challenged children sing, and everyone was moved to tears. Therefore, he said, musical excellence

6. Ibid.

in the worship of God was irrelevant. I responded that had a similarly challenged preacher preached, the congregation would have been similarly moved, but that this does not mean that excellence in preaching is irrelevant. Yes, of course, God rejoiced in the singing of those children, as God does in all of our sincere, best offerings, no matter how meager or mighty our talents may be. This, however, does not excuse those extraordinarily gifted from doing their best for worship, nor does it discount excellence in offerings to God. We are all called, no matter the level of our ability, to offer our very best for the worship of God.

What does it matter what the musician thinks? The pastor is in charge.

The importance of knowledgeable leadership in church music has been addressed above. Parish musicians are not jukeboxes or monkeys to play requested songs for a coin, but are professionals called to make prudent decisions about music for worship. While the pastor is the final authority in most churches, the wise leader will always take seriously the opinion of the person trained in and called for the ministry of music. Any organization and especially churches work best in an atmosphere of mutual trust and respect.

I was at a symphony concert and heard some music that was very moving. Can't we present that in church, so everyone else can be similarly moved?

This is a common idea—that whatever we experience as moving or entertaining should be included in worship. Not

Misconceptions

all emotions, however otherwise good, are appropriate for worship, and hence, not all works of art that may inspire these belong in worship. This is not to say that everything has to be ostensibly sacred to have a legitimate place in worship. There are items, including great literature and art, that may not be overtly sacred, that nevertheless can speak authentically in worship; but for worship, again the "spirits must be tested" (1 John 4:1).

QUALITY IN MUSIC IS SIMPLY A MATTER OF TASTE, AND EVERYONE'S TASTE IS AS GOOD AS ANOTHER'S.

Taste is impossible to codify. However, there are general standards of taste that evolve through groups and cultures. The church at large has developed a canonic style, and, as one guide, I have offered the maxim that all music for worship should commend itself to this tradition. The acknowledgement of any standard would work a miracle of improvement. If congregations actually considered whether particular musical selections and styles were appropriate for their worship, character in worship would take an exponential leap. Many now apparently and unfortunately assume that any music should or could be offered.

Though God loves all people equally, there are more advanced tastes, just as there are more advanced aspects of all areas of human endeavor. Some athletes are better than others, as are some singers, some orators, some inventions, and some pieces of music. However popular the notion may be, all things are not equal. We are called to offer our best for the worship of God, and this best will advance according to our abilities, experience, and commitment.

To attract new worshipers, many churches have begun worship services at nontraditional times. Where done respecting the ancient tradition of the church and the holiness of worship, this is helpful and commendable. Many churches however, believe modern folk don't relate well to a traditional worship venue, so they offer these in places other than their sanctuaries, often in spaces deliberately designed to appear secular. But, how can we abandon our holy sanctuaries, and not present our worship in the presence of the holy of holies? This violates the commandment to keep the Sabbath holy. Granting that these churches believe they are doing the right thing by offering these alternative services, if it turns out that they are not, it does them little good to claim that only part of their congregation is affected. Poor worship exercised in part of the congregation weakens the whole.

Doesn't the gift of music come from God, and thus isn't all music a blessing for worship?

Ideally this is true; but unfortunately God's blessings can be perverted, even unintentionally, to bad purposes. The greater the strength of the blessing—and music is among the most powerful—the greater the potential evil. Hence, not all things made from the materials God gave us are good or efficacious for worship.

Beyond the character of the music selected, the performance style can make the holiest piece appear profane. Imagine a soloist singing "Fairest Lord Jesus" with a huge rock musical taped accompaniment, wearing a bedazzling uniform, and vaunting vocal pyrotechnics accompanied by sensual choreography, all devoid of the natural humility before Christ embodied in the text and tune. This renders the music indiscernible from the music of the world

Misconceptions

and, consciously or not, suggests the worship of Mammon rather than God.

Why are standards important? Aren't all our offerings equally valuable in God's sight?

Some get nervous when standards in worship are brought up. "No one has the right to legislate worship." "We do as the Holy Spirit leads us." I learned early in my career that integrity in worship has to be defended. Testing the spirits is essential to true worship.

Standards are applied in all worship; everyone has them and practices them. To test this, propose to doubters that their church hire the Rockettes, replete with their Rockefeller Center outfits, to perform liturgical dance. "That's ridiculous," you'll hear. "No one would do that." But granting the extreme example nevertheless proves my point. Everyone has standards for worship—but each person has a different set. Part of my objective is to convince us that what we put in worship is so important that it deserves our best thought and practice—our highest standards.

"Offer an acceptable sacrifice" (2 Sam 24:24). We don't take to worship our least offerings; we take our most valuable. The widow's mite, though not much in the eyes of the world, was the most she could offer, a real sacrifice. We need the right heart and spirit, but we also have to offer our best.

This includes the best we ordinary mortals create as well as the best of those whom God made geniuses. Works of genius in music, liturgy, and preaching in the service of worship bring us closer to God and advance God's realm on earth. We value all works in the service of Christ, and rejoice that God inspires some of these to be prophetic.

The God of Abraham, Isaac, and Jacob

> Guard your steps when you go to the house of God; to draw near to listen is better than the sacrifice offered by fools; for they do not know how to keep from doing evil. (Eccl 5:1)

CHURCH SHOULD BE MORE FUN!

Few want to bear the awe and endure the discipline of authentically attending to the worship of God. It is far easier to be treated to a cavalcade of sound-bite lessons, popular sensual miscellany, and clap-happy self-congratulations and thus be entertained through the hour of worship. Coming to church for fun seems more appealing, but departing brings only more of the same, without the transfiguring encounter with God that enables our life in Christ. True worship nevertheless engenders the inherent joy of the life in Christ.

> *How lovely is your dwelling place,*
>   *O Lord of hosts!*
> *My soul longs, indeed it faints*
>   *for the courts of the Lord;*
> *my heart and my flesh sing for joy*
>   *to the living God.* (Ps 84:1–2)

10

God First

Draw near to God, and God will draw near to you.
(Jas 4:8)

The God of Abraham, Isaac, and Jacob

CHAPLAIN VANNORSDALL, WHILE I was a student, gave a sermon illustration that has stuck with me. While a student at Harvard, he learned that when the philosophy building was being built, the dean had asked the faculty to submit a quotation to be inscribed on the façade of the building. They duly considered and, before summer break, submitted, "Man, the Measure of All Things," the words of Protagoras of Abdera. When they returned in the fall, they found, "What is Man that Thou art Mindful of him" (Ps 8:4).

We belong to God; God is our source of life; God is sovereign—ruler of all things seen and unseen. While we have been given minds to comprehend and bodies to overcome, we do not then assume for ourselves those things that are divine, but ever stand in awe of God's inscrutable wisdom and incomprehensible power. Without God, we cannot know and we cannot do. We need not chase vain pursuits, building Babel towers, and anxiously trying to save the church and ourselves.

> *We dance round in a ring and suppose,*
> *But the Secret sits in the middle and knows.*[1]

The secret in the middle is God. Trust in God and God's love for us, and God will show us the way. "Draw near to God and God will draw near to you" (Jas 4:8).

We go to worship to find God. Putting God first, we worship in the manner God has forged with our forebears, and there strive to learn and follow God's will. Absent direct revelations, God's will is divined from scripture and the midrashic tradition, as quickened in the context of particular people in a specific pastoral setting. The midrash set forth in chapter 5 embodies my proposed pastoral-prophetic model, where the tradition shines through living ministry

1. Frost, "Secret Sits," 362.

with God's people. With one foot firmly in the tradition, one may dare reach the other forward, testing unknown ground. Thus when we misstep, we may rock back on theological *terra firma* and then step forward again until we hit prophetic ground. We sing the songs handed down by our forebears, honoring our mothers and fathers, and reach out for new songs and techniques, testing them in the holy midrashic fires. Thus, we have hope of worshiping the God of Abraham, Isaac, and Jacob.

True worship is inherently winsome and we can trust in its appeal to others. However good the motives, luring the unchurched into worship via materials of the world is a bait and switch tactic bound to fail.

> Let no man turn aside, ever so slightly, from the broad path of honor on the plausible pretense that he is justified by the goodness of his end. All good ends can be worked out by good means. Those that cannot are bad, and may be counted so at once, and left alone.[2]

On this subject, Fred Craddock quotes the folk saying, "dance with the one that brung ya," meaning to stick with the ways of our forebears who brought us to faith. Speaking of dancing, as I said in chapter 4, outside of worship, it is not my purpose to discourage wholesome fun: "Earth's the right place for love: I don't know where it's likely to go better."[3]

In chapter 2, I propose that individuals and churches that want to ensure they are following Christ should see that their ministries are rooted in the holy ways of our Christian forebears. We know from false prophets related in scripture that merely invoking Christ's name does not provide this

---

2. Dickens, *Barnaby Rudge*, 399.
3. Frost, "Birches," 122.

The God of Abraham, Isaac, and Jacob

authority. Those abandoning inherited liturgical forms and substituting ways of the world, no matter how large their memberships and no matter what good they otherwise do, risk serving Mammon rather than Christ. As Fred Craddock has said, "If you lean your ladder against the wrong wall, what does it matter how high you climb."

Though some hold that ancient or even decades-old musical forms and songs are no longer relevant and cannot be made to inspire contemporary congregations, if my foregoing logic holds, then the liturgical materials that have evolved through church history are, nevertheless, like Holy Scripture, not only relevant today, but essential for the practice of Christian faith. How are these traditional forms made vital for contemporary worship? In the same way as Holy Scripture. Consider the limitless variance in reading styles of scripture. The same passage can be read on the one hand without understanding, with stumbling inaccuracy, and without feeling, or on the other hand with studied comprehension, heartfelt spirituality, and rhetorical fire. The former will be lifeless, and the latter, whether scripture or music, will be irresistible and prophetic.

Fred Craddock is an example of one, and there are others, who while preaching in traditional forms and liturgical styles, through his expression, disciplined writing, and heartfelt delivery keeps congregations mesmerized, feeling welcomed, and loved. As related in the James Muilenburg quote in chapter 3, encountering the holy inspires a sense of "an inviolable potency outside and beyond, removed and distant, yet at the same time near and 'fascinating.'"[4]

The old forms and songs, when invested with heart and mind, still have the divine spark and yet ring with holy fire. This, of course, requires the sacrificial offering of hard work and strong faith. Those churches undertaking

4. Muilenburg, "Holiness," 616.

this—and there are very many of all sizes and denominations—are reaping God-sent blessings of vital, creative, true worship, often with thriving, growing memberships. Regardless, they have the inherent reward of honoring the gospel. These churches are honoring God's command in Genesis to subdue the world, and are not being subdued by it (Gen 1:28).

As all Christian churches center on the same scripture, so all churches should have a dialectic relationship to the music and liturgy that developed with it—the human-divine language. Thus new songs and styles will be introduced and absorbed into the liturgy, but on terms of respect for the church's liturgical tradition. This process ensures the inculcation of new music without succumbing to the idolatry of pandering to popular culture. Thus over time, through prayerful respect for tradition and consideration of the new, the church's liturgy will deepen and Christians of disparate traditions will draw closer together and toward God.

We are all searching for the place where God reigns, for the Kingdom that Jesus claimed as his own: "My Kingdom is not of this world" (John 18:36). Our forebears have not given us a failsafe formula for finding this kingdom. But they have given us help. They have given us a weekly discipline of worship. They have passed down a commandment to keep the Sabbath holy. And though we know that God can act at any time and place, our scripture tells us that God wants a distinct place to dwell among us—a sanctuary where humans might come in humble awe to encounter the holy of holies. Thus, from ancient times, humans have built sanctuaries where, by mutual appointment, we have met God and where we have shared a common language of worship. Evolving in the divine precincts of worship, this language of worship is unique and therefore distinct from the language of the world. Music that has arisen from this historic divine–human relationship, and that has come from composers whose genius for the divine we recognize, is also part of this distinct language of worship. There, in the sanctuary we have fashioned for the habitation of God, in the finest liturgy we can offer, we experience the transfiguring presence of God. Though we stand in silent awe of the Almighty, our worship is nevertheless warm and social, for, empowered by the Holy Spirit, we listen, pray, sing, and commune spiritually with our sisters and brothers in Christ, inviting the Spirit to blow where it will, even billowing to Pentecostal gales. There, in the beauty of holiness, as much as is possible in this world, we may find the kingdom Jesus speaks of as being "not of this world."

Of course, Jesus did go into the world, and into all strata of society. Once there, however, he did not adopt the ways of the world, but rather transfigured them, reconciling the world unto himself, and bringing the kingdom of this world into the kingdom of God. Similarly, when we move from worship back into the world, we are thereby a little better able to live in and attract others to the kingdom that Jesus claimed as his own.

We look to God, not to the world. In worship, we draw near to God and trust that God will draw near to us. A principal focus on God in worship does not, as some may fear, diminish interaction with society or the representation to the world of the Christian faith. Such contact with the world—and even temptation—may, after all, be essential to human progress toward salvation. As the folk carol "Adam Lay Ybounden" says, "blessed be the time the apple taken was, therefore we moun singen, 'Deo gratias'!" This is part of the mystery of God's gift of salvation through Christ. Further, it is impossible to live and not interact with the non-spiritual world. We need not, therefore, intentionally

God First

introduce secular ways to make worship more relevant or appealing. The inevitability of worldly incursions into spiritual life renders it all the more essential that we keep our times of worship holy and focused on God. Worship is our principal redoubt from the ways of the world and surest avenue to the spiritual life with God.

The holy calling of the worship leader, custodian of the canon, purveyor of the midrash and prophet, is well conveyed in the following excerpt from Nathaniel Hawthorne's *The Marble Faun*. Here Hawthorne speaks of a sculptor and the enduring material of marble, but these speak even more truly to the leader of worship and the timeless and holy disciplines of the worship of God.

> A sculptor, indeed, to meet the demands which our preconceptions make upon him, should be even more indispensably a poet than those who deal in measured verse and rhyme. His material, or instrument, which serves him in the stead of shifting and transitory language, is a pure white undecaying substance. It insures immortality to whatever is wrought in it, and therefore makes it a religious obligation to commit no idea to its mighty guardianship, save such as may repay the marble for its faithful care, its incorruptible fidelity, by warming it with an ethereal life. Under this aspect, marble assumes a sacred character; and no man should dare to touch it unless he feels within himself a certain consecration and a priesthood, the only evidence of which, for the public eye, will be the high treatment of heroic subjects, or the delicate evolution of spiritual, though material beauty.[5]

---

5. Hawthorne, *Marble Faun*, 172–73.

The God of Abraham, Isaac, and Jacob

Thus we commit no liturgical act in worship unless it embodies our most noble aspirations and is imbued and quickened with our heartfelt faith and the Holy Spirit. We offer to God the best of the materials and traditions given us by our forebears and the finest creations, however modest, based on these of our own hearts and minds, using the divine-human language of worship they have passed on to us, and offered in the sanctuary of God in the divine precincts of holy worship. Thus we hope to draw near the God of Abraham, Isaac, and Jacob, and trust that their God—our God—will draw near to us.

Bibliography

Calvin, John. "Epistle to the Reader." In *Source Readings in Music History From Classical Antiquity to the Romantic Era*, edited by Oliver Strunk, 345–48. New York: Norton, 1950.

Chrysostom, St. John. "Exposition of Psalm XLI." In *Source Readings in Music History From Classical Antiquity to the Romantic Era*, edited by Oliver Strunk, 67–70. New York: Norton, 1950.

Craddock, Fred B. "Appalachian Weekend." Opening remarks for Chancel Choir concert, Craddock Center, Cherry Log Christian Church, Cherry Log, GA, September 30, 2006.

Dawn, Marva J. *Reaching Out Without Dumbing Down: A Theology of Worship for This Urgent Time*. Grand Rapids: Eerdmans, 1995.

Dickens, Charles. *Barnaby Rudge: A Tale of the Riots of Eighty*. In *Master Humphrey's Clock*, vol. 2, 229–420. London: Chapman and Hall, 1841.

Frost, Robert. "Birches." In *The Poetry of Robert Frost: The Collected Poems, Complete and Unabridged*, edited by Edward Connery Lathem, 121–22. New York: Holt, Rinehart and Winston, 1969.

———. "The Secret Sits." In *The Poetry of Robert Frost: The Collected Poems, Complete and Unabridged*, edited by Edward Connery Lathem, 362. New York: Holt, Rinehart and Winston, 1969.

Hawthorne, Nathaniel. *The Marble Faun: or, The Romance of Monte Beni*. Boston: Ticknor and Fields, 1860.

Inge, William Ralph. *Diary Of A Dean: St. Paul's 1911–1934*. New York: Macmillan, 1950.

Keck, Leander. *The Church Confident*. Nashville: Abingdon, 1993.

Luther, Martin. "Martin Luther to the Devotees of Music." Preface to *Symphoniae iucundae*, Georg Rhau, 1538. Reprint and translation in *Luther's Works: Liturgy and Hymns*, edited by Ulrich S. Leupold, vol. 53, 321–24. Philadelphia: Fortress, 1965.

MacGimsey, Robert. "Sweet Little Jesus Boy." New York: Carl Fischer, 1934.

Bibliography

Muilenburg, James. "Holiness." In *The Interpreter's Dictionary of the Bible*, edited by George Arthur Buttrick et al, vol. 2, 616–24. Nashville: Abingdon, 1962.

Pagels, Elaine. "The Gospel Truth." *New York Times*, April 8, 2006.

Pius X. "Instruction on Sacred Music." In *Papal Legislation on Sacred Music*, Robert F. Hayburn, 223–24. Collegeville: Liturgical Press, 1979.

Runyon, Theodore. *The New Creation: John Wesley's Theology Today*. Nashville: Abingdon, 1998.

Shaw, Robert. "Worship and the Arts." Lecture given at Memorial Church, Harvard, MA, November 11, 1981. In *The Robert Shaw Reader*, edited by Robert Blocker, 365–78. New Haven: Yale University Press, 2004.

The United Methodist Church. *The Book of Discipline of the United Methodist Church*. Nashville: United Methodist Publishing, 2008.

Watts, Isaac. "Broad is the Road that Leads to Death." In *The Sacred Harp*, edited by B. F. White and E. J. King, 38. Philadelphia, 1844. Reprint of 1859 edition, Philadelphia: S. C. Collins, 1860; facsimile reprint, Nashville: Broadman, 1968.

Wesley, John. *A Pocket Hymn Book, for the use of Christians of all Denominations*. 5th ed. London: 1790.

Wesley, Samuel Sebastian. Introduction to *Musica Britannica: A National Collection of Music*, xv. Vol. 57, *Samuel Sebastian Wesley, Anthems* 1. Edited by Peter Horton. London: Stainer & Bell, 1990.

www.ingramcontent.com/pod-product-compliance
Lightning Source LLC
Chambersburg PA
CBHW070509090426
42735CB00012B/2702